THE WISDOM OF SAINT ISAAC THE SYRIAN

†

SAINT ISAAC THE SYRIAN

GRAPEVINE BOOKS

Published by
GRAPEVINE BOOKS

www.grapevinebooks.com
email: contact@grapevinebooks.com

Ordering Information:
Quantity sales: Special discounts are available on quantity purchases
by corporations, associations, and others.
For details, reach out to the publisher.

First published by Grapevine Books, 2025

Contents

CHAPTER I

GOD, THE UNIVERSE AND HUMANKIND

The world has become mingled with God, and creation and Creator became one!
II/5, **18**

OUR STUDY OF SAINT ISAAC must begin with an investigation of his doctrine of God, the Creator and Guide of the universe, and his understanding of how God reveals himself through the created world. In this connection, Isaac's ontology must also be analyzed, that is, his teaching on the structure of the created being, as must his Christology, the doctrine of the redemption of the world by the incarnate Word of God. This analysis will help us define Isaac's place in the Eastern theological tradition and his interpretation of the christian faith, that is, his personal attitude to fundamental dogmas of Christianity.

1. DIVINE LOVE WHICH REVEALS ITSELF THROUGH THE CREATED WORLD

In Isaac's understanding, God is above all immeasurable and boundless love. The conviction that God is love dominates Isaac's thought: it is the source of his theological opinions, ascetical recommendations, and mystical insights. His theological system cannot be comprehended apart from this fundamental concept.

Divine love surpasses human understanding and verbal description. At the same time, this love is reflected in God's actions with respect to the created world and humankind: 'Among all his actions there is none which is not entirely a matter of mercy, love, and compassion: this constitutes the beginning and the end of his dealings with us'. Both the creation of the world and God's coming to earth in flesh had as its only aim, 'to reveal his boundless love to the world'.

Divine love was the main reason why God created the universe and is the main driving force behind the whole of creation. In the creation of the world divine love revealed itself in its fullness:

What that invisible Being is like, who is without any beginning in his nature, unique in himself, who is by nature beyond the knowledge, intellect, and feel of created beings, who is beyond time and space, being the Creator of these, who at the beginning of time was learnt about through hints and was made known as if it were through his mark by means of the establishing of the fullness of creation, who made his voice heard in connection with his handiwork and so the Being of his lordship was made known, the fountainhead of innumerable natures—this Being is hidden, for as he dwelt in his Being for aeons without number or limit or beginning, it pleased his graciousness and he made a beginning of time, bringing the worlds and created beings into existence. Let us consider then, how rich in its wealth is the ocean of his creative act, and how many created things belong to God, and how in his compassion he carries everything, acting providentially as he guides creation, and how with a love that cannot be measured he arrived at the establishment of the world and the beginning of creation; and how compassionate God is, and how patient; and how he loves creation, and how he carries it, gently enduring its importunity, the various sins and wickednesses, the terrible blasphemies of demons and evil men.

Divine love is a continuing realisation of the creative potential of God, an endless revelation of the Divinity in his creative act. Divine love lies at the foundation of the universe, it governs the world, and it will lead the world to that glorious outcome when it will be entirely 'consumed' by the Godhead:

What profundity of richness, what mind and exalted wisdom is God's! What compassionate kindness and abundant goodness belong to the Creator! With what purpose and with what love did he create this world and bring it into existence! What a mystery does the coming into being of the creation look towards! To what a state is our common nature invited! What love served to initiate the creation of the world! … In love did he bring the world into existence; in love is he going to bring it to that wondrous transformed state, and in love will the world be swallowed up in the great mystery of him who has performed all these things; in love will the whole course of the governance of creation be finally comprised.

The will of God, which is replete with love, is the primal source of all that exists within the universe:

He it is who dwells in the light of his nature, who wished all creation to approach the dark cloud of his eternal glory, who has given the crown of his own everlastingness to the creation which he made,… who has caused the fullness of what he has established to participate in the everlastingness of his Kingdom, Being, and Lord, exalted beyond any secondary notion; whose will is the fountainhead of natures, with the worlds, created beings and natures flowing from him as though from a source, without number or limits.

God is not only the Creator of the universe and its driving force, he is first of all 'the true Father', 'who in his great and immeasurable love surpasses all in paternal affection'. Thus his attitude to the created world is characterized by an unceasing providential care for all its inhabitants: for angels and demons, human beings and animals. God's providence is universal and embraces all. None of his creatures is excluded from the scope of the loving providence of God, but the love of the Creator is bestowed equally upon all:

There is not a single nature who is in the first place or last place in creation in the Creator's knowledge,… similarly there is no before or after in his love towards them: no greater or lesser amount of love is to be found with him at all. Rather, just like the continual equality of his knowledge, so too is the continual equality of his love.

All living creatures exist in God's mind before their creation. And before they were brought into being, they received their place in the hierarchical structure of the universe, a place which is taken away from no one, even if one falls away from God:

Everyone has a single place in [God's] purpose in the ranking of love, corresponding to the form he beheld in them before he created them and all the rest of created beings, that is, at the time before the eternal purpose for the delineation of the world was put into effect. … He has a single ranking of complete and impassible love towards everyone, and he has a single caring concern for those who have fallen, just as much as for those who have not fallen.

The providential care of God and his love extend to angels, who were the first product of the divine creative act, and includes those who fell away from God and turned into demons. According to Isaac, the love of the Creator towards fallen angels does not diminish as a result of their fall, and it is no less than the fullness of love which he has towards other angels.

To think that hatred and resentment exist in God, even against demonic beings, would be thoroughly odious and utterly blasphemous, Isaac claims; as it would be to imagine in that glorious Nature any other weakness or passibility or whatever else might be involved in the retribution of good or bad. Instead, God acts towards us in ways he knows will be advantageous to us, whether by means of things that cause suffering, or by way of things that cause relief, whether they cause joy or grief, whether they are insignificant or glorious: all are directed towards the single eternal good.

To say that the love of God diminishes or vanishes because of a created being's fall would be 'to reduce the glorious Nature of the Creator to weakness and change'. Yet we know that

There is no change or any earlier or later intentions, with the Creator: there is no hatred or resentment in his nature, no greater or lesser place in his love, no before or after in his knowledge. For if it is believed by everyone that the creation came into existence as a result of the Creator's goodness and love, then we know that this original cause does not ever diminish or change in the Creator's Nature as a result of the disordered course of creation.

Nothing that happens in creation may affect the nature of the Creator, Who is 'exalted, lofty and glorious, perfect and complete in his knowledge, and complete in his love'.

This is why God loves the righteous and sinners equally, making no distinction between them. Before creation, God knew humanity's future sinful life, and yet created humankind. God knew all persons before they become righteous or sinners, yet the fact that they underwent change does not change his love. Even many blameworthy deeds are accepted by God with mercy,

and are forgiven their authors, without any blame, by the omniscient God to whom all things are revealed before they happen, and who was aware of the constraints of our nature before he created us. For God, who is good and compassionate, is not in the habit of judging the infirmities of human nature or actions brought about by necessity, even though they may be reprehensible.

Even when God chastises someone, he does so out of love and for the sake of that person's salvation and not for retribution. God respects human free will and does nothing against it:

God chastises with love, not for the sake of revenge—far be it!—but in seeking to make whole his image. And he does not harbour wrath until such time as correction is no longer possible, for he does not seek vengeance for himself. This is the aim of love. Love's chastisement is for correction, but does not aim at retribution. ... The man who chooses to consider God as avenger, presuming that in this manner he bears witness to His justice, the same accuses Him of being bereft of goodness. Far be it that vengeance could ever be found in that Fountain of love and Ocean brimming with goodness!

The image of God as Judge is completely overshadowed in Isaac by the image of God as Love (ḥubba) and Mercy (raḥme). According to him, mercifulness (mraḥmanuta) is incompatible with justice (k'inuta):

Mercy is opposed to justice. Justice is equality on the even scale, for it gives to each as he deserves. … Mercy, on the other hand, is a sorrow and pity stirred up by goodness …; it does not requite a man who is deserving of evil, and to him who is deserving of good it gives a double portion. If, therefore, it is evident that mercy belongs to the portion of righteousness, then justice belongs to the portion of wickedness. As grass and fire cannot coexist in one place, so justice and mercy cannot abide in one soul.

Thus one can speak not at all of God's justice, but of mercy that surpasses all justice:

As a grain of sand cannot counterbalance a great quantity of gold, so in comparison God's use of justice cannot counterbalance his mercy. Like a handful of sand thrown into the great sea, so are the sins of the flesh in comparison with the mind of God. And just as a strongly flowing spring is not obscured by a handful of dust, so the mercy of the Creator is not stemmed by the vices of his creatures.

Decisively rejecting the idea of requital, Isaac shows that the Old Testament understanding of God as a chastiser of sinners, 'visiting the iniquity of the fathers upon the children unto the third and fourth generation', does not correspond with the revelation we have received through Christ in the New Testament. Though David in the Psalms called God 'righteous and upright in his judgments', God is in fact good and merciful. Christ himself confirmed God's 'injustice', in his parables—in particular the parables of the workers in the vineyard and of the prodigal son, and still more so by his incarnation for the sake of sinners: 'Where, then, is God's justice, for while we are sinners Christ died for us?'

Thus, Isaac claims, one should not interpret literally those Old Testament texts, where wrath, anger, hatred, and other similar terms are applied to the Creator. When such anthropomorphic terms occur in Scripture, they are being used in a figurative sense, for God never does anything out of wrath, anger, or hatred: anything of that sort is far removed from his nature. We should not read everything literally, as it is written, but rather perceive within the Old Testament narratives the hidden providence and eternal knowledge of God. 'Fear God out of love for him, and not for the reputation of austerity that has been attributed to him'.

If by nature God is love, someone who has acquired perfect love and mercy towards all creation becomes godlike: his perfect state of love towards creation is a mirror wherein he can see a true image and likeness of the Divine Essence. All the saints 'seek for themselves the sign of complete likeness to God: to be perfect in the love of the neighbour'. Characteristic in this connection is Isaac's well-known text about the 'merciful heart' through which one becomes like God:

And what is a merciful heart? It is the heart burning for the sake of all creation, for men, for birds, for animals, for demons, and for every created thing; and by the recollection of them the eyes of a merciful man pour forth abundant tears. By the strong and vehement mercy which grips his heart and by his great compassion, his heart is humbled and he cannot bear to hear or to see any injury or slight sorrow in creation. For this reason he offers up tearful prayer continually even for irrational beasts, for the enemies of the truth, and for those who harm him, that they be protected and receive mercy. And in like manner he even prays for the family of reptiles because of the great compassion that burns without measure in his heart in the likeness of God.

The 'merciful heart' in a human person is therefore the image and likeness of God's mercy, which embraces the whole of creation, people, animals, reptiles, and demons. In God, there in no hatred towards anyone, but all-embracing love which does not distinguish between righteous and sinner, between a friend of truth and an enemy of truth, between angel and demon. Every created being is precious in God's eyes. He cares for every creature, and everyone finds in him a loving Father. Even if we turn away from God, God does not turn away from us: 'If we believe not, yet he abideth faithful, for he cannot deny himself'. Whatever happens to humankind and to the whole of creation, however far it may remove from God, he remains faithful to it in his love, which he cannot and will not deny.

2. THE STRUCTURE OF THE CREATED WORLD

According to biblical revelation, creation comprises both the invisible world of bodiless spirits and the visible material world. To the former belong angels and demons; to the latter the whole universe, including human beings, animals, and inanimate objects.

Isaac summarizes the biblical account of creation in the following passage:

On the first day eight noetic natures were created, seven in silence and one by verbal command, and this was light; on the second day the firmament was created; on the third day God gathered the waters and made the herbs to blossom forth; on the fourth day, the division of light; on the fifth day, the birds, reptiles and fish; and on the sixth day, the animals and man.

In speaking of the structure of the angelic world, Isaac expounds on the ninefold angelic hierarchy, a teaching borrowed from the Corpus Areopagiticum, which is in turn based on the names of angelic beings encountered in the Old Testament. Referring to the biblical text, Isaac says:

The divine books have given all these spiritual essences nine spiritual names and divided them into three divisions of three each. The first is composed of the great, sublime and most holy Thrones, the many-eyed Cherubim, and the six-winged Seraphim; the second in order is composed of the Dominions, the Virtues and the Powers; the third is composed of the Principalities, the Archangels and the Angels. The names of the orders are thus interpreted: in Hebrew Seraphim means those who are fervent and burning; the Cherubim, those who are great in knowledge and wisdom; the Thrones, receptacles of God and rest... . These orders are given these names because of their operations. The Thrones are so called as once truly honoured; the Dominions, as those who possess authority over every kingdom; the Principalities, as those who govern the atmosphere; Powers, as those who give power over the nations and every man; Virtues, as once mighty in power and dreadful in appearance; the Seraphim, as those who make holy; the Cherubim, as those who carry; the Archangels, as vigilant guardians; the Angels, as those who are sent.

Isaac tells us that God created angels 'all of a sudden, out of nothing' as worlds on high without number, limitless powers, legions of seraphs of fire, fearful and swift, wondrous and mighty, which have the power to carry out the will of the almighty design, the simple spirits which are luminous and incorporeal, which speak without a mouth, which see without any eyes, which hear without any ears, which fly without any wings. ... They do not tire or grow feeble, they are swift in movements, never delaying in any action, fearful to look upon, whose ministry is wondrous, who are rich in revelations, exalted in contemplation, who peer into the place of the Shekhina of Invisibleness, glorious and holy essences, who are arranged in ninefold order by the Wisdom which has created all. ... They are fiery in their movements, acute in intellect, wondrous in knowledge, resembling God insofar as that is possible.

Thus angels resemble God and within themselves bear his likeness: 'In them Being, the Creator who is above all things, constituted a resemblance in everything—as far as possible—to himself. Angels, Isaac says, are 'invisible beings, whose task it is to be stirred by praises of God in that great stillness which is spread over their world, so that, by these praises, they may be raised up in contemplation to the glorious Nature of the Trinity, and remain in wonder at the vision of the majesty of that ineffable glory'. Angels are always astonished at the divine mysteries, 'because of revelations that come upon them in various ways'.

Demons, on the other hand, are 'extremely polluted', and in their state of uncleanness they cannot see the angelic orders that are above them. Demons possess the same qualities as angels, but the divine light is not given to them, as they are bearers of darkness. The demons will to ruin and destroy a human being; yet they cannot do any harm to him unless they have permission from God. Thus demons are entirely subject to God and they act only in accordance with God's permission and order. In particular, when we are attached to God night and day, God allows neither demons nor wild animals and reptiles to hurt us in any way: 'rather, in our presence they behave in complete peacefulness, as ministers of God's will'. But if we are attached to sin, God gives the order to one of the demons to 'flog us harshly', not out of revenge, but so that 'by one means or another we will not become lost far away from God'.

If the invisible world of angels has been created with the aim of praising God's glory and might, the material world also is called to bear witness to God's omnipotence. The material world has been made as a magnificent temple that reveals and reflects God's beauty. Isaac's cosmology corresponds to the scientific conceptions of his time: God laid out the earth as a bed and heaven as 'a vault'; he fixed 'the second heaven as a wheel that adheres to the first heaven'; he created the ocean that surrounds heaven and earth 'as a girdle'; 'therein he established lofty mountains reaching even to heaven, and he ordered the sun to journey behind the mountains all the night long; he set the great sea within the mountains and it dominates over one-half and one-fourth of the dry land'.

The human person is also created as a temple of God, a dwelling place of the Divinity. The indwelling of God within this temple was most fully realized in the person of Christ—God who became man. We shall speak more specifically later of Isaac's Christology and of his understanding of the deification of human nature by Jesus Christ. Here we want only to point out that human nature, in Isaac's vision, is created with the potential of accommodating the fullness of the Divinity. Human nature has also the potential for endless existence, in the likeness of God. Every human person is provided with five 'incomparably great gifts': life, sense perception, reason, free will, and authority. In speaking of the structure of a human person, Isaac follows the division of human nature into spirit, soul, and body which is traditional in greek philosophical and patristic anthropology. He also maintains the division of the soul into three parts—desire, zeal, and reason (reḥmta, ḥnana, mliluta, corresponding to the Greek to epithymitikon, to thymoeides, to logistikon). This concept, derived from platonic anthropology, he borrowed from Evagrius, John the Solitary, and Babai.

We do not find in Isaac a developed doctrine of the fall and original sin, which, according to christian tradition, led to the loss of the initial god-likeness of human beings and damaged and perverted the whole of human nature. Isaac's teaching on the passions and sin, however, fully corresponds to that doctrine. According to him, God did not impose the passions and sin upon our nature. The passions are characteristic of humans in their fallen state. By its nature, the soul is dispassionate. In its original nature, the soul was characterized by godlike dispassion; only later did the passions entered into the soul. Both the body and the soul became subject to the passions when they lost what belonged to them by their nature and went outside their well-being.

At the same time, as if contradicting himself, Isaac claims that there are passions which are given by God: these passions of the body and soul are implanted in them for their benefit and growth. This apparent contradiction is clarified by the fact that the syriac word ḥašša, like its greek counterpart pathos, means both 'passion' and 'suffering'. Thus, the sinful passions are unnatural, whereas the sufferings sent by God may serve to promote spiritual growth. Isaac's teaching is also clarified by reference to the patristic tradition, in which there are two understandings of pathos: a sinful desire of the soul; and a natural capacity of the soul which can be directed towards both good and evil. Isaac may have had in mind both understandings of 'passion' as he wrote the texts quoted above.

Unlike the sufferings which come from God, the sinful passions harm human nature. 'Anyone who does not voluntarily withdraw himself from the causes of the passions is involuntarily drawn away by sin', Isaac warns. 'These are the causes of sin: wine, women, riches, and robust health of body. Not that by their nature these things are sins, but rather nature readily inclines towards the sinful passions on their account, and for this reason man must guard himself against them with great care'.

3. THE INCARNATION

After the fall, humanity's only means of turning away from the passionate towards the original blessed state comes through the Incarnation of the Word of God. The Incarnation, which stands at the centre of the New Testament message, is one of the key themes of Saint Isaac.

Because Isaac expounded his Christology in accordance with east-syrian theological tradition, where the use of 'nestorian' terminology is characteristic—it is in fact the terminology of Theodore of Mopsuestia, inherited by his disciple Nestorius—a good number of Isaac's christological texts were never translated into Greek and thus remained unknown till the present. The only work of the 'Greek Isaac' that deals directly with christological matters is the 'Epistle to Symeon', but it belongs, as we have said, to Philoxenus of Mabbug and thus contains a Christology opposed to Isaac's. Only after the rediscovery of Part II does a precise analysis of Isaac's Christology become possible. But before turning to the newly-discovered texts, let us first point to a few characteristic passages from Part I in which some christological themes are mentioned.

Here we find the Incarnation identified as the moment when the love of God for human beings reveals itself to the highest degree and when human beings are called, in turn, to respond to the love of God with their own love for God:

God the Lord surrendered his own Son to death on the cross for the fervent love of creation. ... Yet this was not because he could not redeem us in another way, but so that his surpassing love, manifested hereby, might be a teacher unto us. And by the death of his Only-begotten Son he made us near to himself. Yea, if he had had anything more precious, he would have given it to us, so that by it our race might be his own. Because of his great love for us it was his pleasure not to do violence to our freedom, although he is able to do so, but he chose that we should draw near to him by the love of our understanding. For the sake of his love for us and obedience to his Father, Christ joyfully took upon himself insult and sorrow. ... In like manner, when the saints become perfect, they all attain to this perfection, and by the superabundant outpouring of their love and compassion on all men, they resemble God.

The Incarnation took place, then, because of the love of both the Father and of the Son for human beings, and because of the Incarnation a human person is able to attain such a state of love when he becomes like God.

The Incarnation of the Son of God is, according to Isaac, the new revelation about God. In Old Testament times, before the Incarnation, people were unable to contemplate God and to hear his voice, but after the Incarnation this became possible:

Creation could not look upon him unless he took part of it to himself and thus conversed with it, and neither could it hear the words of his mouth face to face. The sons of Israel were not even able to hear his voice when he spoke with them from the cloud... . The sons of Israel made ready and prepared themselves, keeping themselves chaste for three days according to the command of Moses, that they might be made worthy of hearing the voice of God, and of seeing the vision of his revelation. And when the time was come, they could not receive the vision of his light and the fierceness of the voice of his thunder. But now, when he poured out his grace upon the world through his own coming, he has descended, not in an earthquake, not in a fire, not in a terrible and mighty sound, but 'as the rain upon a fleece, and rain-drops that fall upon the earth', softly, and he was seen conversing with us after another fashion. This came to pass when, as though in a treasury, he concealed his majesty with the veil of his flesh, and among us spoke with us in that body which his own bidding wrought for him out of the womb of the Virgin.

Not only for human beings, but also for angels, the door of contemplation and vision was opened in Jesus when the Word became flesh; before the Incarnation they could not penetrate into these mysteries, Isaac claims.

In Part I we also find a passage in which Isaac discusses how the two natures of Christ are shown in Holy Scripture. According to him, Scripture often uses words figuratively. For example, 'things that pertain to the body are said of the soul', and vice versa.

Likewise things pertaining to the Lord's Divinity, which are not compatible with human nature, are said with respect to his all-holy body; and again, lowly things are said concerning his divinity which pertain to his humanity. Many, not understanding the intent of the divine words, have stumbled here with a stumbling from which there is no recovery.

Under the 'many' Isaac most probably means the monophysites: as a true diophysite, he insists upon the necessity of distinguishing between the divine and human natures of Christ, in spite of the fact that Scripture does not make such a precise distinction.

These are the main christological passages from Part I. When we turn to Part II we direct our attention first to one of the 'Gnostic Chapters' in which Isaac speaks of the Incarnation. He emphasizes that God's love for creation was the main and only reason of the coming on earth of the Son of God and of his death on the cross:

If zeal had been appropriate for putting humanity right, why did God the Word clothe himself in the body, using gentleness and humility in order to bring the world back to his Father? And why was he stretched out on the cross for the sake of sinners, handing over his sacred body to suffering on behalf of the world? I myself say that God did all this for no other reason than to make known to the world the love that he has, his aim being that we, as a result of our greater love arising from an awareness of this, might be captivated by his love when he provided the occasion of this manifestation of the kingdom of heaven's mighty power—which consists in love—by means of the death of his Son.

The Incarnation and the death on the cross of the Saviour, Isaac claims, happened not to redeem us from sins, or for any other reason, but solely in order that the world might become aware of the love which God has for his creation. Had all this astounding affair taken place solely for the purpose of forgiveness of sin, it would have been sufficient to redeem us by some other means. What objection would there have been if he had done what he did by means of an ordinary death? But he did not make his death at all an ordinary one—so that you might realize the nature of this mystery. Rather, he tasted death in the cruel suffering of the cross. What need was there for the outrage done to him and the spitting? Just death would have been sufficient for our redemption— and in particular his death, without any of these other things which took place. What wisdom is God's! And how filled with life! Now you can understand and realize why the coming of our Lord took place with all the events that followed it, even to the extent of his telling the purpose quite clearly out of his own holy mouth: 'God so loved the world that he gave his only-begotten Son'—referring to the Incarnation and the renewal he brought about.

Therefore, it was the love of God, and not the necessity of redeeming humanity from sin, which was the sole reason for the Incarnation of the Word. God became man because he wanted human beings to turn to him as their father. Isaac speaks of this in Chapter XL:

When the entire extent of creation had abandoned and forgotten God and had perfected themselves in every kind of wickedness, of his own will and without any supplication or request from elsewhere he came down to their abode and lived among them in their body just as one of them, and with a love exalted beyond knowledge or description by any created being, he begged them to turn back to himself, showing them concerning the glorious establishment of the world to come, having intended before all worlds to introduce felicity such as this for creation: he informed them of its existence and forgave them all the sins which they had previously committed, and confirmed this good will by means of authoritative signs and wonders, and the revelation to them of his Mysteries; and finally he has stooped down so far that he is willing to be called 'Father' of sinful human nature, dust from the earth, despicable human beings, flesh and blood: can these things be performed without great love?

Let us now look at Chapter XI, in which the Christology of Isaac is expounded with great precision. In this chapter, which is largely dedicated to the cross, our attention is drawn by the abundance of typically east-syrian terms through which Isaac presents his christological ideas. The cross, he says, is a symbol of 'the Man who completely became a temple' of God; the cross is made in the name of 'that Man in whom the Divinity dwells'; the humanity of Christ is the 'garment of his Divinity'. The use of such terms is characteristic of the entire east-syrian tradition, which can be designated as strongly dyophysite. The humanity of Christ had already been described by Ephrem as a 'garment', a phraseology preserved by later east-syrian writers, but subsequently expunged in the west-syrian tradition.

Following a tradition derived from Theodore of Mopsuestia and Diodore, Isaac emphasizes that, although Christ has two natures, we venerate them together, that is, we worship one Christ in two natures. In doing so, we ascribe to the man Jesus the same names that are ascribed to God the Word:

We do not hesitate to call the humanity of our Lord—he being truly man—'God' and 'Creator' and 'Lord'; or to apply to him in divine fashion the statement that 'by his hand the worlds were established and everything was created'. For he to whom all these things apply willingly dwelt in him, giving him the honor of his divinity and authority over all, because of the benefits which creation was about to receive through him. ... He even bade the angels worship him, according to the words of the blessed Paul: 'introducing the Firstborn into the world, he said: Him shall all the angels of God worship'. He granted to him that he should be worshipped with himself indistinguishably, with a single act of worship for the Man who became Lord and for the Divinity equally, while the two natures are preserved with their properties, without there being any difference of honor.

Therefore God 'willingly dwelt' in the man Jesus; whereas the man Jesus 'became' God and by his death on the cross received power over the whole of creation. Because of the cross, the man Jesus was lifted up to God the Word:

For we believe that all that applies to the Man is raised up to the Word who accepts it for himself, having willed to make him share in this honor. All this is made known to us in the cross, and through this affair, which unbelievers consider so contemptible, we have acquired an accurate knowledge of the Creator.

This strongly diophysite understanding of the person of Jesus Christ may appear to lead in the theological thought of Isaac to a division of the image of the historical Jesus. But this is not the case. Isaac understands Christ as one person: God who came in human flesh. The humanity of Christ is as real as the humanity of each one of us. At the same time the man Jesus is simultaneously God the Word and the Creator of the universe:

O wonder! The Creator clothed in a human being enters the house of tax collectors and prostitutes, and when they turn towards him—through his own action—he was urging them, providing them, by means of his teaching, with assurance and reconciliation with him. And he sealed the word of truth with true testimonies, consisting in miracles and signs. Thus the entire universe, through the beauty of the sight of him, was drawn by his love to the single confession of God, the Lord of all, and so the knowledge of the one Creator was sown everywhere.

The universal significance of the coming of God on earth and dwelling in human flesh is thus clearly emphasized.

What are the soteriological consequences of Isaac's christological accent on the distinction between the two natures of Christ? Does it not imply a rejection of the belief—which is traditional in Eastern Christian theology—that the salvation of humanity occurs through deification of the human nature and that this takes place because of the union of human nature with the divine in the person of Christ? In the alexandrian tradition, in particular, deification was understood as occurring through the unity of the two natures in Christ: as iron, in being united with fire, turns into fire, so humanity, united with the Divinity, becomes deified. If there is no real unity and there is only a conditional unity 'in veneration', how can anyone speak of the deification of human nature?

Isaac, who did not use the alexandrian terminology of deification, appears not to have rejected the idea of deification, but he expressed it in a different way. According to him, the man Jesus, upon ascending to God after his resurrection, raised human nature up to the level of the Divinity. Furthermore, the suffering, the death, the resurrection and the ascension of Christ opened up to human nature the possibility of ascending to God:

Amid ineffable splendour the Father raised him to himself to heaven, to that place where no created being had trod, but to which he had, through his own action, invited all rational beings—angels and human beings—to that blessed Entry, in order to delight in the divine light in which was clothed that Man who is filled with all that is holy, who is now with God in ineffable honour and splendour'.

This approach to soteriology differs from the alexandrian; but does not lose the essence of the christian message: the salvation of the human being by Christ through the unity of human nature with the Divinity. The way by which the man Jesus ascended— from earth to heaven, from humanity to Divinity—is opened up to everyone after his resurrection. Deification is perceived dynamically, as an ascent of the human being, together with the whole created world, to divine glory, holiness and light.

In addition to Chapter XI, another very important text in connection with Christology is Chapter V of Part II, which also contains several characteristic passages. There we find a prayer using the terminology of a 'temple' and 'the one who dwells in it':

I give praise to your holy Nature, Lord, for you have made my nature a sanctuary for your hiddenness and a tabernacle for your mysteries, a place where you can dwell, and a holy temple for your Divinity, namely, for him who holds the sceptre of your kingdom, who governs all you have brought into being, the glorious Tabernacle of your eternal Being, the source of renewal for the ranks of fire which minister to you, the Way to knowledge of you, the Door to the vision of you, the summation of your power and great wisdom—Jesus Christ, the only-begotten from your bosom and remnant gathered in from your creation, both visible and spiritual.

The idea of the human person ascending to God through the Incarnation of the Word is also present in this prayer: 'O Mystery exalted beyond every word and beyond silence, who became human in order to renew us by means of voluntary union with the flesh, reveal to me the path by which I may be raised up to your mysteries ...' The terminology of 'voluntary union', which occurs in both Nestorius and Babai, is generally characteristic of the east-syrian tradition.

The Incarnation is understood as the sacrifice of God the Son which was offered because God the Father loves the world and which united the created world with God. Isaac speaks of the union of God with the world as a 'mingling', an expression which would never be allowed by the east-syrian tradition in connection with the natures of Christ:

You have given your entire treasure to the world: if you gave the only-begotten from your bosom and from the throne of your Being for the benefit of all, what further do you have which you have not given to your creation? The world has become mingled with God, and creation and Creator have become one!

Is this statement about the 'mingling' between the world and God not a way of overcoming of the extremes of the dyophysitism? In other words, this statement breaks down the sharp boundaries between God and creation which are a characteristic of the strongly diophysite position of the Church of the East. If Theodore of Mopsuestia and his disciples can be accused of making a distinction between the divine and human natures which leads to a division of the image of Christ into two, can we maintain that in Isaac the Syrian, who represents the same stream of theological thought, we find a break with the extremes of diophysitism? Isaac does not speak of the essential unity, let alone a 'confusion', of the two natures of Christ. He does, however, speak of the 'mingling' of God with creation, and this implies that the sharp demarcation between divinity and humanity that was strongly present in the school of Theodore is not equally strong in Isaac.

Precisely because the uncreated Word of God and the created man Jesus are one and the same person, Isaac finds it possible to speak of the 'mingling' (ḥultana) of God with the creation through the Incarnation of God the Word. Thus in his prayer Isaac appeals to Christ as to one person who is simultaneously God and man:

O Christ who are covered with light as though with garment, who for my sake stood naked in front of Pilate, clothe me with that might which you caused to overshadow the saints, whereby they conquered this world of struggle. May your Divinity, Lord, take pleasure in me, and lead me above the world to be with you. O Christ, upon you the many-eyed Cherubim are unable to look because of the glory of your countenance, yet out of your love you received spit upon your face: remove the shame from my face and grant an open face before you at the time of prayer.

In summarizing what has been said of the theology of Isaac the Syrian, we emphasize yet again that his entire theological thought derives from the idea that God reveals himself to the world as ineffable love. This love created the world and guides it. Out of love for creation and for the salvation of humankind, God assumed human flesh and died on the cross that he might renew human nature and open for humanity an entrance into the kingdom of heaven. The salvation of a human person is nothing else than an ascent to the divine light and love; it is a following of Christ, who was a human being, but was raised up to the level of the Divinity, and by this deified human nature.

CHAPTER II

THE WAY OF A SOLITARY

Love all men, but keep distant from all men.

I/64 (314) = PR 65 (457)

AMONG THE CHARACTERISTIC TRAITS of Saint Isaac the Syrian's asceticism we shall look at in this chapter, we begin with his understanding of the ascetical life as one lived in solitude, far from the world and the passions. We shall explore his teachings on the renunciation of the world required of a Christian when he enters the ascetic way; on the love of God and neighbor; on stillness as one of the main conditions for achieving peace of the mind. While we will emphasize various aspects of monastic and solitary life, we shall also touch on some of Isaac's more general ideas concerning christian life, in particular his teaching on the fulfillment of God's commandments and the struggle against the passions. This survey should allow us to see Isaac's individuality as an ascetical writer and to appreciate the originality of his approach to some key themes of christian asceticism.

1. SOLITUDE AND RENUNCIATION OF THE WORLD

The hero in Isaac's writings is the ihidaya, the 'solitary' or, literally, 'single one'. In Isaac's day, this term (related to Hebrew yahid, 'single') was used to designate a solitary monk, as opposed to dayraya, a cenobitic monk. The initial meaning of the term, however, points much more broadly to the unity of a human person within himself and to his unity with God. Thus in the Peshitta, the term ihidaya was used as a title for Adam as created after the image of one God: 'It was wisdom which preserved the ancestral father, the ihidaya, who had been created in the world'. In the New Testament ihidaya is first of all the epithet of Jesus Christ, translating Greek monogenes, 'the Only-Begotten'. In syriac writings of the fourth century the term was already being used to refer to ascetics, those who are like angels in that they do not marry. A solitary is someone who lives in Christ, 'the Only-Begotten (ihidaya) from the Father who gives joy to all solitaries (ihidaye)', as Aphrahat says.

Solitude is not for Isaac a synonym for celibacy and the eremitical life. It is first and foremost an experience of union with God. Most people find loneliness burdensome, taking it as a fully negative experience of isolation, abandonment, the absence of 'the other' with whom they might share the joys and sufferings of earthly existence. For Isaac, on the contrary, loneliness is an experience of the presence of God, who is closer to him than any friend and who always cares for him. '... God has never perceptibly shown his action except in a region of stillness, in the desert, and in places bereft of chance encounters with men and of the turbulence of their habitations'. If someone lives in the desert, far from people, one should be sure that there is with him a Guardian who will never leave him alone. The soul of the person who is separated from the world and leads the life of stillness is lifted up toward God: astonished, it is struck with wonder and remains with God.

Solitude is the internal experience of living within oneself, of withdrawal into one's inner person—a necessary action for uniting oneself with God. At the same time, it is the experience of renouncing the 'other', even a friend or a relative. It is, finally, an experience of withdrawal from the world and renunciation of it for the purpose of achieving union with God. Solitude can be painful, fraught with inner suffering, but without the experience of solitude one can never come close to the fullness of life in God.

Thus, according to Isaac, renunciation of the world for the sake of a solitary life in God is a necessary condition for entering upon the way to God. 'Liberation from the material things precedes the bond of God'. Again, 'No one can draw nigh to God save the man who has separated himself from the world. But I call separation not the departure from the body, but departure from the world's affairs'. The 'world' in this context is 'a collective noun which is applied to the so-called passions'. To go out of the world and to die to the world means to liberate oneself from passions and 'the mind of the flesh', that is, from everything bodily and material which puts obstacles in the way of the spiritual life. Love of the world is incompatible with love of God; one needs to liberate oneself from the first in order to acquire the second: 'The soul that loves God finds rest only in God. First detach yourself from all external bonds and then you may strive to bind your heart to God, because unification with God is preceded by detachment from matter'.

Renunciation of the world is a gradual process which begins with a desire to attain contemplation of God. Renunciation includes the discipline of both the body and the mind. There is a correspondence between the degree of one's renunciation and one's ability to enter the contemplation of God:

Blessed is the majesty of the Lord who opens the door before us, so that we may have no other wish save desire for him! For thus do we abandon all things and our mind goes forth in quest of him alone, having no care which might hinder it from the contemplation of the Lord. The more the mind takes leave of care for the visible and is concerned with the hope of future things, my beloved brothers,... the more it is refined and becomes translucent in prayer. And the more the body is freed from the bonds of worldly affairs, the more the mind is also freed from the same. ... Therefore the Lord gave us a commandment that before all else a man should hold fast to non-possessiveness and should withdraw from the turmoil of the world and release himself from the cares common to all men. He said: 'Whosoever forsaketh not his entire human state and all that belongeth to him, and renounceth not himself, cannot be my disciple'.

This ideal of total renunciation of the world was embodied in practice in early eremitical monasticism. Because they wished avoid the struggle arising from the proximity of worldly things, the ascetics of the past withdrew into the desert:

... As long as a man does not remove himself from what his heart dreads, his enemy always has a point of vantage against him. ... Because our ancient Fathers, who walked these paths, knew fully well that our intellect is not at all times in vigorous health, ... they with wisdom considered the matter, and clad themselves with non-possessiveness as a weapon. ... They have gone out into the desert, where there is nothing which can be an occasion for the passions. ... I mean they would have no occasion for anger, lust, the remembrance of wrongs, and glory, and that both these and their like would be at a minimum by reason of the desert. For they walled themselves up in the desert as in an impregnable tower. Thus each of them was able to finish his struggle in solitude, where the senses find no help for assisting our adversary through encounter with hurtful things.

Monks flee from the world, therefore, to avoid occasions of encountering the passions, sins, and sinful thoughts. But apart from this there is in eremitical monasticism a quest for a renunciation of people which in some cases leads a solitary to total rejection of any encounter with them. This flight, too, is undertaken for the sake of union with God: the solitary does not want anyone to distract him from God. Isaac has very strong words about the harm which may be done to a solitary through encounters with people:

O, how evil is the sight of men and intercourse with them for solitaries! … For just as the sudden blast of ice falling on the buds of the fruit-trees nips and destroys them, so too, contacts with men, even though they be quite brief and to all appearances done to a good purpose, wither the bloom of virtue—newly flowering due to the temperate air of stillness—which covers with softness and delicacy the fruit-tree of the soul planted beside the channels of the waters of repentance. And just as the bitterness of the frost, seizing upon new shoots, consumes them, so too does conversation with men seize upon the root of a mind that has begun to sprout the tender blades of the virtues. And if the talk of those who have controlled themselves in one particular thing, but who in another have minor faults, is apt to harm the soul, how much more will the chatter and sight of ignoramuses and fools …?

Speaking of the necessity of fleeing the world and people, Isaac often cites as examples the ancient ascetics. Arsenius the Great, who was especially dear to him, observed a commandment given to him by God: 'Arsenius, flee men and be saved'. Once, seeing a visitor approaching his desert, Arsenius ran away from him. 'Wait for me, father', the monk cried, 'because I am running after you for God's sake'. 'And I for God's sake am fleeing you', Arsenius replied. On another occasion Arsenius fell down before a monk who came to see him, declaring: 'I shall not get up until you have departed'. When an archbishop came to ask him for spiritual instruction, he answered: 'Whenever you hear that Arsenius is found, do not draw nigh to that place'. Being asked by Abba Macarius about his reason for avoiding people, Arsenius replied: 'God knows that I love you, but I cannot be with both God and men'.

The renunciation of people, Isaac taught, should be radical and absolute. Any bond of relationship, friendship, or love should be severed. The renunciation of relatives is a traditional theme in monastic literature. In developing it, Isaac refers to the example of a saintly monk who never visited his brother, also a monk. When the brother was about to die, he sent word to him, asking to come to bid him farewell.

But the blessed man was not persuaded, not even at that hour when nature is wont to be compassionate to other men and to overstep the limit set by the will. He said: 'If I go out, my heart will not be pure before God… .' And his brother died and did not see him.

This refusal may seem cruel by contemporary standards, but it shows the degree of renunciation required of monks in early monasticism.

To achieve fullness in his life in God, a monk should be able to forget other people, to restrain himself from care about them and from acts of mercy:

If you wish to hold fast to stillness, become like the Cherubim, who take no thought for anything of this life, and fix in your mind that no one else exists on the earth but you and God whom you heed, even as you have been taught by the fathers who lived before you. Unless a monk hardens his heart and forcibly restrains his compassion so as to become distant from solicitude for all other men, either for God's sake or for some material need, and he perseveres only in prayer during the times which he has appointed without having affection and concern for others enter his heart, he will be unable to attain freedom from turbulence and cares and to live in stillness.

Though the point here is refraining from acts of mercy during times appointed for prayer, Isaac clearly considered the life of stillness higher than activity on behalf of people. He insisted upon the necessity of renouncing philanthropic activity, at least during certain periods of time.

2. LOVE OF GOD AND LOVE OF ONE'S NEIGHBOUR

How does this radical insistence on the renunciation of people correspond to the commandment to love one's neighbour? Is this flight from people not a flight from Christ himself, who said: 'Thou shalt love thy neighbour as thyself'? Does this self-isolation not lead to a loss or an absence of love for people, to selfish indifference towards anyone except oneself?

Isaac would reply in the negative. On the contrary, he says, flight from people paradoxically leads to an increased love of them. The commandment to love God is universal and it embraces the commandment to love one's neighbour:

The commandment which says, 'Thou shalt love the Lord thy God with all thy heart, and with all thy soul, and with all thy mind', more than the world, nature, and all that pertains thereto, is fulfilled when you patiently endure in your stillness. And the commandment that speaks of the love of neighbour is included within the former. Do you wish to acquire in your soul the love of your neighbour according to the commandment of the Gospel? Separate yourself from him, and then the heat and flame of love for him will burn in you and you will rejoice at the sight of his countenance as though you beheld an angel of light. And do you wish that those who love you should thirst for you? See their faces on fixed days only. Truly, experience is the teacher of all.

We should emphasize here, for the sake of readers who find this attitude towards other people shocking, that Isaac was not here giving recommendations which would be universally applicable. His writings are addressed primarily to solitaries, and he is usually talking to a very specific readership. Moreover, he speaks only of his own experience as a solitary by vocation, and of the experience of other solitaries, those around him and those of past ages. At issue is the specifically monastic way of learning to love people by giving up all encounters with them.

Isaac is convinced that the main task of a Christian is the purification of his inner person: this is more important than contact with people or any activity on their behalf. Such activity is especially dangerous when the soul of a monk is not yet purified and the passions are not yet extirpated from it. There were many people, Isaac says, who were known for their deeds of philanthropy, but because they dwelt constantly in the world, with its passions and temptations, they failed to take sufficient care for their own souls:

Many persons have accomplished mighty deeds—raised the dead, toiled for the conversion of the erring, and wrought great wonders; and by their hands they have led many to the knowledge of God. Yet after doing these things, these same people who quickened others fell into vile and abominable passions and killed themselves, becoming a stumbling-block for many once their action was manifest. For they were still sickly in soul, and instead of caring for their soul's health, they cast themselves into the sea of this world in order to heal the souls of others, but being yet in ill health, in the manner I have stated, they lost their souls and fell away from their hope in God. The infirmity of their senses was not able to confront or resist the flame of things which customarily drive the vehemence of the passions wild.

Isaac does not reject good deeds. He simply points to the necessity of being spiritually healthy before going into the world to heal others. One can bring more profit to others when one is spiritually strong and has acquired experience of the inner life. External activity is no substitute for inner depth, not even an apostolic activity which is indeed very useful to others:

It is an excellent thing to teach men what is good and by constant care to draw them away from delusion and into the knowledge of life. This is the path of Christ and the apostles, and it is very lofty. But if a man perceives within himself that by such a way of life and continual communion with men his conscience is being weakened by seeing external things, his serenity is being disturbed, and his knowledge is being darkened, … and that while he seeks to heal others he is losing his own health and, departing from the chaste freedom of his will, his intellect is being shaken; then let him … turn back, lest he hear from the Lord the words of the proverb, 'Physician, heal thyself'; let him condemn himself, let him watch over his own good health. Instead of audible words let his excellent manner of life serve as an education, and instead of the sounds of his mouth let his deeds teach others, and when he keeps his soul healthy, let him profit others and heal them by his own good health. For when he is far from men he can benefit them even more by the zeal of his good works than by his words, since he is himself sickly and in greater need than they of healing. For 'If the blind lead the blind, both shall fall into the ditch'.

The solitary, according to Isaac, must first heal his own soul and only then care for the souls of others. Inner life in God is more important than any philanthropic and missionary activity:

Love the idleness of stillness above providing for the world's starving and the conversion of a multitude of heathen to the worship of God. It is better for you to free yourself from the shackle of sin than to free slaves from their slavery. It is better for you to make peace with your soul … than by your teaching to bring peace among men at variance. For, as Gregory the Theologian says, 'It is a good thing to speak concerning the things of God for God's sake, but it is better for a man to make himself pure for God'…. It is more profitable for you to attend to raising up unto the activity of intuitions concerning God the deadness of your soul due to the passions than it is resurrecting the dead.

This does not mean that Isaac disapproved of works of charity in general. He simply emphasized that these works are not the hermits' primary task: they are more appropriating for laymen. Christians in the world should do charitable work; the hermits' first task is to look after their own inner thoughts and purify their intellect:

For the fulfilling of the duty of love with respect to providing for physical well-being is the work of those in the world, or even of monks, but only those who are imperfect, who do not dwell in stillness, or who combine stillness with brotherly concord and continually come and go. For such men this is good and worthy of admiration. Those, however, who have chosen to withdraw from the world in body and in mind,... should not serve in the husbandry of physical things and visible righteousness. ... Rather, by mortification of their members which are upon the earth—after the apostolic utterance—they should offer God the pure and blameless sacrifice of their thoughts, the first-fruits of their husbandry, and also the affliction of their bodies by their patient endurance of perils for their future hope. For the monastic discipline rivals that of the angels. It is not right for us to abandon this celestial husbandry and to cleave to material things.

Speaking outside the context of the eremitical life, Isaac emphasizes the necessity of good deeds done for the sake of one's neighbour. He objects to the words of a certain monk who says that 'monks are not obliged to give alms': only that monk, Isaac says, is not obliged to do so who 'possesses nothing upon the earth, who earns nothing for himself among material things, who in his mind clings to nothing visible, and does not endeavour to acquire anything'. Cenobitic monks are not released from the necessity of giving alms and performing acts of philanthropy for their neighbour. As for hermits, they cannot give alms, but they must have mercy, which should be revealed not so much in good deeds as in prayer which takes in the whole world. At the same time deeds cannot be avoided, especially if the situation requires immediate action for the sake of someone who is suffering:

'Blessed is the merciful man, for he shall obtain mercy', not only in the hereafter, but also here in a mystical way. Indeed, what mercy is greater than this, that when a man is moved with compassion for a fellow man and becomes a partaker in his suffering? Our Lord delivers his soul from the gloom of darkness—which is the noetic gehenna—and brings her into the light of life, thus filling her with delight. ... And when it is in your power to deliver the iniquitous man from evil, do not neglect to do so. I do not mean that if the affair is far removed from you, you should go and throw yourself into the work of this sort, for deeds of this kind do not belong to your way of life. If, however, the affair is placed directly into your hands and is within your power,... then take heed to yourself, lest you become a partaker of the blood of the iniquitous man by not taking pains to deliver him. ... Instead of an avenger, be a deliverer. Instead of a faultfinder, be a soother. Instead of a betrayer, be a martyr. Instead of a chider, be a defender. Beseech God on behalf of sinners that they receive mercy.

Even hermits, whose task is not to perform good deeds, should act as deliverers and defenders of people in some situations. In general, they should strive to obtain love of their neighbour as an inner quality, to acquire a universal merciful love towards every human being and every creature. Through being merciful they may heal their own souls, Isaac says, making an important addendum to his own opinion that good deeds should not be performed before one's soul is healed. While good deeds cannot heal the soul of the person doing them, the inner mercy does heal his soul:

Let the scale of mercy always be preponderant within you, until you perceive in yourself that mercy which God has for the world. Let this our state become a mirror wherein we may see in ourselves that likeness and true image which naturally belong to the Divine Essence. By these things and their like we are enlightened so as to be moved toward God with a limpid intellect. A harsh and merciless heart will never be purified. A merciful man is the physician of his own soul, for as with a violent wind he drives the darkness of passions out of his inner self.

This universal love about which Isaac speaks cannot be obtained by deeds of philanthropy or, in general, by human effort: it is a gift which we receive directly from God. Isaac's teaching on how the love of neighbour is acquired can be outlined as follows: a person withdraws himself from his neighbour for the sake of life in solitude and stillness; through this he acquires an ardent love of God; this love gives birth in him to the 'luminous love' (ḥubba šapya) of humanity.

This term is borrowed by Isaac from the Macarian Homilies, John the Solitary and other syrian writers. The theme of 'luminous love' is developed by Isaac in Chapter X of Part II:

A person who has stillness and converse of knowledge will easily and quickly arrive at the love of God, and with the love of God he will draw close to perfect love of fellow human beings. No one has ever been able to draw close to this luminous love of humanity without having first been held worthy of the wonderful and inebriating love of God.

The scheme offered by Isaac is therefore different from the one we find in the First Epistle of John: 'He that loveth not his brother whom he hath seen, how can he love God whom he hath not seen?' According to Isaac, one should first love God whom he does not see and by means of this love draw near to the love of his neighbour whom he sees—or in this case whom he also does not see because he has deliberately withdrawn from seeing him. To acquire the love of one's neighbour by means of good deeds is as impossible as acquiring the love of God by means of the love of neighbour:

To come from the toil and struggle with the thoughts to the luminous love of humanity, and from this to be raised up to the love of God—is a course impossible for someone to complete in this life, right up to the time he departs from the world, however hard he struggles. On the basis of the commandments and by discernment, it is possible for someone to control his thoughts and to purify his sensibility with respect to [others], and he can even perform good towards them. But for him to attain to a luminous love of humanity by means of struggle, I am not persuaded to admit as possible: there is no one who has attained this, and none who will attain it, by this path in life. Without wine no one can get drunk, nor will his heart leap with joy; and without inebriation in God, no one by the natural course of events will obtain the virtue that does not belong to him, nor will it remain in him serenely and without compulsion.

At issue here is a special and the highest form of love of one's neighbour, which Isaac calls 'luminous' and 'perfect' and which is a gift from God. It does not belong to human nature and is therefore not a natural love of human beings, domestic animals, birds, wild animals, and so on, which we encounter in some people; it is a supernatural love which is born from 'inebriation' in the love of God.

The 'luminous love' of neighbour is that sacrificial love which makes one like God, who loves sinners and righteous equally:

In the case of the person who has been deemed worthy to taste of divine love (ḥubba alahaya), that person customarily forgets everything else by reason of its sweetness, for it is something at whose taste all visible things seem despicable: such a person's soul gladly draws near to a luminous love of humanity, without distinguishing [between sinners and righteous]; he is never overcome by the weakness to be found in people, nor is he perturbed. He is just as the blessed Apostles were as well: people who in the midst of all the bad things they endured from the others were nonetheless utterly incapable of hating them or of being fed up with showing love for them. This was manifested in actual deed, for after all the other things they accepted even death so that these people might be retrieved. These were men who only a little bit earlier had begged Christ that fire might descend from heaven upon the Samaritans just because they had not received them into their village! But once they had received the gift and tasted the love of God, they were made perfect in love even for wicked men: enduring all kinds of evils in order to retrieve them, they could not possibly hate them. So you see that perfect love of fellow human beings cannot be found just as a result of keeping the commandments.

Taking the Gospel's teaching about the two greatest commandments as his base, therefore, Isaac offers his own interpretation. He sets out his own path for attaining to the love of God and neighbour. But this path is not for the majority of people who live in the world: it is only for those who have chosen solitude as a way of life, who have renounced the world and who draw near to God by means of life in stillness.

Living far from people and remaining internally alone, one can and must show love to others:

Rejoice with the joyous and weep with those who weep; for this is the sign of limpid purity. Suffer with those who are ill and mourn with sinners; with those who repent rejoice. Be every man's friend, but in your mind remain alone. Be a partaker of the sufferings of all men, but keep your body distant from all. Rebuke no one, revile no one, not even men who live very wickedly. Spread your cloak over the man who is falling and cover him. And if you cannot take upon yourself his sins and receive his chastisement in his stead, then at least patiently suffer his shame and do not disgrace him. … Know, brother, that the reason why we must remain within the door of our cell is to be ignorant of the wicked deeds of men, and thus, seeing all as holy and good, we shall attain to purity of mind.

The luminous love of neighbour is born from the heart that is purified and the mind that dwells in stillness and is totally freed from worldly affairs.

3. STILLNESS AND SILENCE

What is the 'stillness' (šelya), of which Isaac so often speaks? It is a deliberate denial of the gift of words for the sake of achieving inner silence, in the midst of which a person can hear the presence of God. It is standing unceasingly, silently, and prayerfully before God. It is withdrawal from every activity of word and thought in order to attain to stillness and peace of mind.

And this is the definition of stillness (d-šelya): silence (šelyuta) to all things. If in stillness you are found full of turbulence, and you disturb your body by the work of your hands and your soul with cares, then judge for yourself what sort of stillness you are practising, being concerned with many things in order to please God! For it is ridiculous for us to speak of achieving stillness if we do not abandon all things and separate ourselves from every care.

Isaac identifies two types of stillness: outward and inward. Outward stillness consists in keeping the tongue and mouth silent; inward is the silence of the intellect, peace of thought, stillness of heart. Inward stillness is higher than outward, but when inward stillness is lacking, the other is useful: 'If you cannot be still within your heart, then at least still your tongue'. Inward stillness is deepened by outward stillness; and the ascetic should always strive after the second in order to achieve the first:

Love silence above all things, because it brings you close to fruit that the tongue cannot express. Let us force ourselves to be silent and then, from out of this silence is born something that leads to silence itself [i.e. inner silence]. God grant you may perceive some part of that which is born of silence! If you begin with this discipline, I know not how much light will dawn on you from it. Do not infer, O brother, from what is said of that wondrous man Arsenius, that when the fathers would visit him and the brethren come to see him, and he would sit with them and remain silent, and in silence let them go—do not infer, I say, that he did this completely voluntarily, except at the beginning, when he forced himself to it. After a time a certain sweetness is born in the heart out of the practice of this labour, and it leads the body by force to persevere in stillness. ... Silence is also a way to stillness. ... When Arsenius found that it was often impossible, because of the place of his abode, to be far withdrawn from the proximity of men and from the monks who settled in those parts—then by grace he learned this way of life: unbroken silence. And if out of necessity he ever opened his door to some of them, they were gladdened only by the mere sight of him; but conversation with words, and its employment, were rendered superfluous between them.

An experience of silence as the absence of words is an experience of participation in the life of the world to come. As Isaac says, 'silence is a mystery of the age to come, but words are instruments of this world'. Outward silence brings inner fruits, whereas failure to guard the tongue leads to spiritual darkening:

If you guard your tongue, my brother, God will give you the gift of compunction of heart so that you may see your soul, and thereby you will enter into spiritual joy. But if your tongue defeats you,... you will never be able to escape from darkness. If you do not have a pure heart, at least have a pure mouth ...

The nature of inner stillness will be discussed specifically in Chapter VII, where the subject will be 'stillness of mind', one of the highest states of spiritual progress. For the moment we confine ourselves to pointing out the various inner fruits of the 'life of stillness', that is, the eremitical monastic life. Isaac deals with this question in a letter he sent to an anonymous friend. In it Isaac collects testimonies on the fruits of stillness from the ascetics of his time. These testimonies point to different fruits of the life of stillness; in particular:

How this life is conducive to concentration of mind and a deepening of the spiritual activity of the intellect: 'The profit which I gain from stillness is this: when I depart from the dwelling wherein I abide, my mind is void of the preparations of war and turns to a superior activity'.

How this life leads one to spiritual sweetness, joy, inner tranquillity, and an ecstatic loss of sensory and logical activity: 'I run to stillness so that the verses of my reading and prayer should become sweet to me. And when my tongue becomes silent because of the sweetness that comes from understanding them, then, as if into a kind of sleep, I fall into a state in which my senses and my thoughts become inactive. When by prolonged silence my heart becomes tranquil and undisturbed,... waves of joy ceaselessly burst forth to delight my heart. And when these waves approach the barque of my soul, they plunge her into veritable wonders in the stillness which is in God.'

How stillness erases those memories which are harmful to the mind; and how because of this the mind is able to return to its natural state.

How stillness helps one free the mind and concentrate on repentance and prayer: 'When a man sees different faces and hears many kinds of voices foreign to his spiritual rumination,... his mind will not be free so that he can see himself in secret, remember his sins, demolish his thoughts, pay attention to what befalls him, and attend to hidden prayer'.

How stillness assists one 'to bring the senses into submission to the sovereignty of the soul'.

The life of stillness and silence leads to the awakening within the person of that 'hidden man of the heart' of which Saint Peter speaks. This process develops proportionately to the degree of mortification of the outward person, who exists amidst the struggles of this world:

Stillness, as Saint Basil says, is the beginning of the soul's purification. For when the outward members cease from their outward activity and from the distraction caused thereby, then the mind turns away from distractions and wandering thoughts that are outside its realm and abides quietly within itself, and the heart awakens for the searching out of deliberations that are within the soul. And if purity is nothing else save forgetting an unfree mode of life and departing from its habits, how and when will a man purify his soul who, actively of himself or through others, renews in himself the memory of his former habits ...? If the heart is defiled every day, when will it be cleansed from defilement? But if he cannot even withstand the action upon him of outward things, how much less will he be able to purify his heart, seeing that he stands in the midst of the camp and every day hears urgent tidings of war ...? If, however, he should withdraw from this, little by little he will be able to make the first inner turmoils cease. ... Only when a man enters stillness can his soul distinguish the passions and prudently search out her own wisdom. Then the inner man also awakens for spiritual work and day by day he perceives the hidden wisdom which blossoms forth in his soul. ... Stillness mortifies the outward senses and resurrects the inward movements, whereas the outward manner of life does the opposite, that is, it resurrects the outward senses and deadens the inward movements.

Isaac is very consistent in emphasizing the priority of inward over outward activity. At the same time, he makes readers aware that without outward silence of tongue, senses, and thoughts, one cannot achieve inward stillness of mind. So 'the silence for all' becomes the first law of the spiritual life. Without this a person is unable, not only to reach the state of perfection, but even to begin on his pathway to God.

4. A MONASTIC WAY TO GOD

Isaac the Syrian regards the christian life as a way whose goal is union with God. Borrowing Saint Paul's metaphor, Isaac uses the image of a runner in the stadium to describe how the human intellect moves towards that spiritual enjoyment of Christ which is the crown of the solitary life. Sometimes spiritual life is compared with sailing in the sea. But much more often it is described as an ascent by ladder, a very traditional image in christian literature. According to Isaac, this ascent is endless, as its aim is the unbounded God:

The limit of this journey is so truly unattainable that even the saints are found wanting with respect to the perfection of wisdom, because there is no end to wisdom's journey. Wisdom ascends even till this: until she unites with God him who follows after her. And this is the sign that the insights of wisdom have no limit: that wisdom is God himself.

The only way of ascent to God known to Isaac through experience was the monastic and eremitical life. It is therefore not surprising that his ascetical recommendations were addressed primarily to monks, even though many of them are universally applicable. The beginning of life with God is described as making a covenant (qyama) to separate oneself from the world:

For when a man comes unto God, he makes a covenant with God to separate himself from these things. And these are the things I mean: not to look on the face of a woman; not to look on magnificent things or magnificent persons and their luxury, nor on elegant persons and their clothing; not to behold the society of men of the world, nor to hear their words, nor to inquire concerning them.

The question is not so much of monastic vows as of the inner determination to renounce the world and everything worldly, to withdraw completely from human society.

The 'covenant' with God is one of the most prominent themes in syriac proto-monastic literature. It was given a particular development by Aphrahat, who mentions an ascetic group within the Syrian Church, 'the covenanters' (bnai qyama), literally 'sons of the covenant'. These lay people's life was no different from that of other syrian Christians, except for their vows of virginity, poverty, and service to the parish community. At a later time the notion of 'covenant' was transferred to syrian monasticism, which developed the ascetical aspirations of the 'covenanters'. In particular, the idea of the separation of the 'chosen' from others, which loomed large in the spirituality of the 'covenanters', received its full development in the later monastic tradition to which Isaac belonged.

In the latter, monasticism sets itself apart from the rest of humanity; the monks regard themselves as a society of the chosen ones:

By this the sons of God are set apart from the rest of mankind: they live in afflictions, but the world rejoices in luxury and ease. For it is not God's good pleasure that those whom he loves should live in ease while they are in the flesh. He wills rather that, so long as they are in this life, they abide in affliction, in oppression, in weariness, in poverty, in nakedness, isolation, want, illness, degradation, buffetings, contrition of heart, bodily hardship, renunciation of relatives, and sorrowful thought. He wants them to possess an aspect differing from that of the rest of creation, a habitation unlike that of the rest of men, and to live in a solitary and quiet dwelling, unknown to the sight of men and bereft of every gladdening thing of this life. They mourn, but the world laughs; they are sombre, but the world is joyous; they fast, but the world lives in pleasure. They toil by day, and by night they compel themselves to ascetic struggles in straitness and weariness.

Even within christian society monasticism plays a very special role. It is a kind of small church within the Church. Thus every monk should be blameless in his life and a good example for people living in the world:

The monk (ihidaya, solitary) ought in his appearance and in all his actions to be a sight of stimulation to those who see him, so that by reason of his many virtues, which shine forth like sun-beams, the enemies of truth, when they look upon him, will involuntarily confess that the hope of salvation which the Christians have is firm and unshakeable, and from every side will run to him as to a refuge … For the boast of the Church is the monastic way of life.

Monastic way of life is an unseen martyrdom undergone for the sake of receiving the crown of sanctification. It is 'taking up the cross' and thus incompatible with seeking ease: 'The path of God is a daily cross. No one has ascended into heaven by means of ease …' Taking up the cross means participating in the suffering of Christ: 'O straggler, taste within yourself Christ's suffering, that you may be deemed worthy of tasting his glory. For if we suffer with him, then we are glorified with him. The intellect is not glorified with Jesus, if the body does not suffer together with Jesus'. The whole earthly life is perceived by the monk as a self-crucifixion:

As long as you have hands, stretch them out to heaven in prayer, before your arms fall from their joints, and though you desire to draw them up, you will not be able. As long as you have fingers, cross yourself in prayer, before death comes to loose the comely strength of their sinews. As long as you have eyes, fill them with tears before that hour when dust will cover your black clothes …

The way to God is different for each individual monk, but the starting point is the same for everyone: asceticism that includes prayer and fasting. Isaac ascribes an important role to fasting and other means of disciplining the body:

Fasting, vigil and wakefulness in God's service, renouncing the sweetness of sleep by crucifying the body throughout the day and night, are God's holy pathway and the foundation of every virtue. Fasting is the champion of every virtue, the beginning of the struggle, the crown of the abstinent, the beauty of virginity and sanctity, the resplendence of chastity, the commencement of the path of Christianity, the mother of prayer, the well-spring of sobriety and prudence, the teacher of stillness, and the precursor of all good works. Just as the enjoyment of light is coupled with healthy eyes, so desire for prayer accompanies fasting that is practiced with discernment. … And the Saviour also, when he manifested himself to the world in the Jordan, began at this point. For after his baptism. … he fasted for forty days and forty nights. Likewise all who set out to follow in his footsteps make the beginning of their struggle upon this foundation.

Fasting should accompany spiritual activity. Bodily labour, according to Isaac, precedes the labour of the soul, which, in turn, precedes all spiritual activity:

Works performed with the body precede those performed with the soul. … The man who has not performed bodily works cannot possess the works of the soul, since the latter are born of the former as the ear of corn comes from a naked grain of wheat. And the man who does not possess the works of the soul is bereft of spiritual gifts.

Mortification of the body is conducive to spiritual renewal of the soul: 'To the same extent that the body dries up and grows feeble … so the soul is renewed day by day and flourishes through progress towards God …' But there is no profit in bodily labours if they are not accompanied by 'inward ministry of mind' or if a monk restricts his spiritual life to them. The monk who relies only on external ascetical efforts is like the

Pharisees, whom Christ condemned:

The constant limitation of hope which is a feature of merely an outward ministry belongs to the immature and jewish way of thinking of those who boast on their fasts, their tithes, and the length of their prayers, as our Lord says, not possessing inwardly any thought of spiritual awareness or right reflection on God to adorn their interior state with an increase of hope.

In a classical pattern derived from such earlier writers as Evagrius Ponticus and John the Solitary, the monastic way to God is divided into the three stages of spiritual advancement. Following this scheme, Isaac writes:

The stages through which man advances are three: the beginner's stage, the intermediate, and that of the perfect. In the first stage all a man's thinking and recollection is held within the passions, even if his mind is directed toward good. The second is a kind of midway point between passion and the spiritual state: both thoughts from the right hand and those from the left move equally within it, and light and darkness never cease from welling forth.

The third stage is characterized by the revelations of divine mysteries, when God opens his door to a monk for his perseverance in labours.

Accordingly, there are three different types of spiritual labour, each corresponding to a certain stage of spiritual advancement:

The manner and aim of spiritual labour is not the same for the initial stage as for the intermediary one or for the concluding stage. The initial stage involves labouring with a great deal of recitation and simply 'treading out' the body by means of laborious fasting. The intermediary culminating point lessens the amount of all this, exchanging persistence in these for persistence in other things, labouring on spiritual reading and especially on kneeling. The culminating point of the third stage lessens persistence along the lines of the previous stage, labouring instead on meditation and on prayer of the heart.

This does not mean that it is only the beginners who should keep fasting, the intermediate who should read the Scriptures, and the advanced who should pray. The same types of spiritual activity are accomplished by ascetics at all stages throughout their whole life. At the beginner's stage, however, the accent on bodily labours is characteristic; at the stage of perfection the inner activity of mind is more suitable:

It is not that each of these culminating points completely leaves behind the labours characteristic of the previous stage; rather they make an alteration in the aim and manner in which they are performed ... To the middle stage belongs the recitation of the psalms and the labour of fasting; but this is not done without discernment or in an impetuous way, as happens at the initial level. Likewise, even at the perfect culminating point, there is reading and the labour of kneeling and psalmody—but more important than them is persistent meditation on God's providence (mdabbranuta) together with hidden prayer, seeing that there is no longer any need for a great quantity of the former, since after only being occupied with them for a short while, a person is seized by, and remains in wonder.

In the pages that follow we shall speak about various aspects of the inward activity of the mind, discussing separately different sorts of prayer and such mystical phenomena as 'wonder' and contemplation. In the meantime, let us draw some brief conclusions on the way to God Isaac describes. It is a way of ascent from an outward activity of the body to the heights of inward contemplative activity when one is deemed worthy of mystical 'wonder' and union with God. To attain this, one must first renounce the world and be alone with God. One must achieve the inward stillness of mind and heart which is born of the outward silence of the mouth and of solitude. The renunciation of the world and life in solitude do not mean a denial of the love of one's neighbour: on the contrary, by means of this renunciation and withdrawal a person participates in the love of God, which becomes the reason for the awakening within him of the 'luminous love' of his fellow human beings. In short, the life of the solitary Isaac describes moves from outward asceticism to inward contemplation of God; from silence of mouth to stillness of intellect; from solitude to union with God; from outward activity for the sake of people to the 'luminous love of humanity'.

———————————

CHAPTER III

TRIALS ON THE WAY TO GOD

God does not grant a great gift without a great trial.

I/42 (209) = PR 39 (298)

I myself have had many experiences of these things, and what I have discovered is along the lines of what I have indicated here as a reminder, out of brotherly love, since many, I think, are benefitted by these experiences.

II/33,3

ISAAC THE SYRIAN, while best known for his descriptions of the high mystical states characteristic of ascetics who have reached spiritual perfection, does not overlook the negative aspects of christian life—the ordeals and sufferings through which an ascetic has to pass.

In this chapter we shall analyze Isaac's teaching on the difficulties of the christian ascetic life and make an attempt to summarize the negative experiences described in the pages of his works. First, we shall speak of the various temptations which are endured by the ascetic who travels towards God, and, second, of abandonment by God, which is the highest form of suffering.

1. TEMPTATIONS

The syriac term nesyona, which corresponds to the greek peirasmos, can be translated as 'temptation', 'trial', 'ordeal', 'examination', or 'test'; a related word nesyana means 'experience'. Both are related to the hebrew root nsh, which means 'to put on trial, to test'.

In the Bible, we find several types of temptations. Involved in them are three persons: God, a human being, and the devil. God 'tempts' Abraham in order to test his faith; God tests his chosen people in the 'furnace of affliction'; He 'tries the hearts and reins' of people; He 'searches all inward parts of the belly'. The devil, on the other hand, tempts Adam and Eve, urging them to eat from the tree of knowledge; he tempts Jesus in the desert. There is also a third type of temptation—when a human person tempts God: in their disbelief, the people of Israel tempted God; the Pharisees and Herodians tempted Jesus; Ananias and Sapphira tempted the Holy Spirit. Finally, in a fourth type of temptation, a human being is 'tempted when he is driven away out of his own lust'.

Normally, Isaac the Syrian speaks of the two first types of temptation—that coming from God and that coming from the devil. In the first case, it is a question of the experience which is necessary for attaining to knowledge of God; in the second, of what a Christian should fear and try to avoid. Isaac was asked how the words of Christ, 'Pray that ye enter not into temptation,' fit in with Christ's own constant admonitions to bear temptations and afflictions. Isaac answered:

Pray, he says, that you enter not into temptations of your faith. Pray that through your mind's self-esteem you enter not into temptation with the demon of blasphemy and pride. Pray that you enter not by God's permission into the manifest temptations of the senses, which the devil knows how to bring upon you when God permits it because of the foolish thoughts you entertain. … Pray that you enter not into temptations of soul through doubts and provocations by which the soul is violently drawn into great conflict. Even so, prepare yourself with all your soul to receive bodily temptations; voyage in them with all your members and fill your eyes with tears, so that the angel who guards you does not depart from you. For without trials God's providence is not seen, and you cannot obtain boldness before God, nor learn the wisdom of the Spirit, nor can divine longing be established in you. Before temptations man prays to God as though he were a stranger; but when he enters into temptations for the sake of his love and does not permit himself to be deflected, then straightway he has, as it were, God as his debtor, and God reckons him as a true friend, since he had warred against his enemy and defeated him for the sake of his will. This is to 'pray that you enter not into temptation'. And again, pray that you enter not into the fearsome temptation of the devil by reason of your arrogance, but because you love God, and you wish that his power might help you and through you vanquish his enemies. Pray that you enter not into such trials because of the folly of your thoughts and works, but rather in order that your love of God may be tested, and that his strength be glorified in your patience.

Those trials which come from God are sent with the aim of healing the illnesses of the soul. Through bearing temptations a person is drawn near to God and his faith is strengthened:

By the experience of many interventions of divine assistance in temptations, a man also acquires firm faith. Thenceforward he has no fear, and he gains stout-heartedness in temptations from the training he acquired. Temptation is profitable for every one. … Ascetic strugglers are tried, that they may add to their riches; the slothful are tried, that they may thereby guard themselves from what is harmful to them; the sleepy are tried, that they may be armed with wakefulness; those who are far away are tried, that they may draw nearer to God; those who are God's own are tried, that with boldness they may enter into his house. … There is no man who will not feel oppressed at the time of training. And there is no man who will not find bitter the time when he is given the virulent potion of trials to drink. Without temptations a man cannot acquire a strong constitution …

Temptations are sent by God so that in the midst of them one might feel the closeness of God and his providence. When a person put his hope firmly in God, then God sends temptations in order to bring him closer:

As soon as divine grace has made his thinking secure, … so that he puts his confidence in God, she begins, little by little, to introduce him to temptations. She permits him to be sent temptations suited to his measure, that he may bear their force. But in these very temptations her aid palpably draws near him, that he may take courage until little by little he gains experience, acquires wisdom, and holds his enemies in contempt because of the confidence he has in God. For it is not possible without temptations for a man to grow wise in spiritual warfare, to know his Provider and perceive his God, and to be secretly confirmed in his faith, save by virtue of the experience which he has gained. … For God's marvelous love of man is made known to him when he is in the midst of circumstances that cut off his hope; herein God shows his power by saving him.

It is amidst temptations, afflictions, and struggles that one can find God, not in ease and slackness. Isaac speaks of bearing temptations as sailing in rough seas: when the voyage is over and a person reaches the promised haven, he thanks God for the tribulations he has had to endure. Isaac also compares an ascetic with a diver who searches for pearls at the bottom of the sea—a profession whose dangers were familiar to him since he came from Qatar on the Red Sea:

If the diver found a pearl in every oyster, then everyone would quickly become rich! And if he brought one up the moment he dove, without waves beating against him, without any sharks encountering him, without having to hold his breath until he nearly expires, without being deprived of the clear air granted to everyone and having to descend to the abyss—if all this were the case, pearls would come thicker and faster than lightning flashes!

The closer a person comes to God the higher the intensity of temptations rises: this is a law of the spiritual life.

As long as you are journeying in the way to the city of the kingdom [Isaac writes] and are drawing near the city of God, let this be for you a signpost: the strength of the temptations you encounter. The nearer you draw and progress, the more temptations multiply against you. Whenever you perceive in your soul diverse and intensified temptations in your path, therefore, know that at that time your soul has in fact secretly entered a new higher level, and that grace has been added to her in the state where she was found; for God leads the soul into the afflictions of trials in exact proportion to the magnificence of the grace which he bestows.

Isaac emphasizes that God does not send us temptations which would exceed our ability to bear: he always adjusts the force and quantity of them to human strength. But if a person is unable to bear great temptations, he will also not be able to receive great gifts: this is another law of the spiritual life.

If a man's soul has an infirmity and it does not have strength enough for great temptations, and it therefore asks not to enter into them, and God heeds this, then know for a certainty that insofar as the soul is insufficient for great trials, in the same measure it is insufficient for great gifts; and insofar as great temptations are prevented from entering upon the soul, to the same degree great gifts are withheld from it. For God does not grant a great gift without a great trial. In his wisdom, which is beyond the understanding of his creatures, God has ordained that gifts be bestowed in proportion to temptations.

At the same time, Isaac claims, God will not send someone great trials unless He has prepared him by divine grace to bear them. In the combination of temptations and gifts of grace there is a certain dynamic:

Question: Does, then, the trial come first and afterward the gift, or the gift first and the trial follow behind it?

Answer: A trial does not come unless the soul has first secretly received both a portion greater than the measure which it had formerly received and the Spirit of grace. The Lord's temptation and the trials of the apostles testify to the truth of this, for they were not permitted to enter into temptation until they had received the Comforter. It is fitting that those who partake of good should endure also their trials, because their affliction is mingled together with the good. ... If it be so, therefore, that a gift is before trial, nevertheless it is certain that for the testing of a man's freedom, his awareness of temptations precedes his awareness of a gift; for grace never enters a man before he has tasted temptations. Hence, in reality grace comes first, but in the awareness of the senses, it delays to manifest itself.

What is the difference between trials coming from God and those due to the activity of the devil? The trials from God are sent to 'the friends of God, that is to say, the humble'. The friends of God are placed in trials, not in punishment, but with a view to their spiritual progress. These trials are acts of divine pedagogy:

The trials inflicted by the paternal rod for the soul's progress and growth, and those whereby it may be trained, are the following: sloth, oppressiveness of the body; enfeeblement of the limbs; despondency; confusion of mind; bodily pains; temporary loss of hope; darkening of thoughts; absence of human help; scarcity of bodily necessities, and the like. By these temptations a man's soul feels herself lonely and defenseless, his heart is deadened and filled with humility, and he is trained thereby to come to yearn for his Creator. Yet divine providence proportions these trials to the strength and needs of those who suffer them. In them are mingled both consolation and griefs, light and darkness, wars and aid. … This is the sign of the increase of God's help.

By contrast, temptations that come from the devil are sent to 'the enemies of God, that is to say, the proud': these temptations 'fall upon the men who are shameless' and who in their pride abuse God's goodness. Temptations of this sort may exceed the limit of human strength and lead to a spiritual fall. Isaac divides temptations from the devil into two categories: those afflicting the soul and the body. To the first he ascribes 'the withdrawal of the forces of wisdom which men possess, the piercing sensation of the thought of fornication,… quick temper, the desire to have one's own way, disputatiousness, vituperation, a scornful heart, an intellect completely gone astray, blasphemy against the name of God, absurd notions that are ridiculous, or rather lamentable'. To the temptations of the body belong

painful adversities, always prolonged, intricate, and difficult to resolve; constant encounters with wicked and godless men; falling into the hands of men who afflict us; the heart's being suddenly, irrationally, seized by terror; many times stumbling severely on rocks, and having grave falls from high places, and similar mishaps which do the body great injury; and, finally, the heart's being entirely destitute of reliance upon God's care and of the confidence of its faith.

Those Christians who truly love God prove their love by bearing temptations and are strengthened in love: they are tested, like gold in fire, and by this testing become friends of God. On the contrary, those who do not love God 'fall away as dross, since giving way to the enemy they leave the field of battle laden with guilt, either because of the laxity of their mind or because of their pride. They were not worthy to receive the power that the saints had working with them …' In this way, temptations reveal who is a friend and who is an enemy of God, who is faithful and who is not. Temptations are therefore that 'crisis', a judgment before the Last Judgment, where the separation of the sheep from the goats takes place.

A person who tempts God by his pride and laxity can be delivered into the hands of the devil for a trial or temptation. In this case God's anger flames up against him:

You have not yet experienced the sternness of the Lord, when he changes from his right hand, full of kindness, to his left hand, exacting his due to those who abuse him—how angry he burns, and how filled he is with zeal at the time when this has been aroused. He will not turn back, even though you beg him at length, once he has been aroused to this; rather, he burns like a furnace in his anger.

It is very rare for Isaac to speak of God's anger—which does not mean a punishment or requital for sins. As we saw in Chapter I, the idea of divine requital was totally alien to Isaac: God is not angry at someone because he feels insulted or because he burns with the desire of vengeance. Rather he shows visible signs of anger, changing from his right hand to the left, so that a human person can experience the feeling of abandonment and may then be converted to God with a whole heart.

It is precisely for this purpose that one can be 'delivered unto Satan for the destruction of the flesh'. The devil cannot tempt a person at all unless this is allowed by God. There is then a certain 'accord' between God and the devil concerning the limits within which the latter can act. The devil 'asks' God for people, as he 'asked' to put the righteous Job on trial, but it is entirely up to God's power whether or not to deliver someone for trial. Therefore, both the temptations that come from God and those that come from the devil are allowed by God and so can serve one's salvation and spiritual progress.

According to Isaac, the devil has four methods of warring against ascetics. First, at the very beginning when someone enters the way to God, the devil inflicts upon him grave and strong temptations, so that by means of them he may bring the aspiring ascetic to the abyss of despair and turn him from his chosen path. Second, the devil waits a while and when the ascetic's initial zeal grows cold the devil approaches him. Third, the devil observes that an ascetic has made good progress in the spiritual life and then sows in his mind the thought that his success can be ascribed to himself and not to God. Fourth, the devil tempts an ascetic with something to which he is inclined by nature—stimulating in his intellect, for example, thoughts of fornication or various illusions. 'The devil and tempter is allowed to make war upon the saints in all these ways of temptation, so that thereby their love of God may be proven...'

Temptations from God and temptations from the devil can, therefore, both be useful to an ascetic and give him a chance of proving his love for God. Isaac invites every Christian to prepare himself to bear temptations. Without them, no one can make progress in virtues:

Whenever you wish to make a beginning in some good work, first prepare yourself for the temptations that will come upon you, and do not doubt the truth. For it is the enemy's custom, whenever he sees a man beginning a good mode of life with fervent faith, to confront him with diverse and fearful temptations. ... It is not that our adversary has such power—for then no one could ever do good—but that God concedes it to him, as we have learned with the righteous Job. Therefore prepare yourself manfully to encounter temptations ...

2. EXPERIENCE OF ABANDONMENT

Isaac describes the ascetical life as a constant fluctuation between periods of 'assistance' and 'feebleness', presence and abandonment, spiritual ups and downs:

Thus in this way the variation between assistance and feebleness takes place for a person at all times and at all stages in the ascetic life: it may be in the battles waged against chastity, or in the varied states of joy and of gloom; for sometimes there are luminous and joyous stirrings, but then again all at once there is darkness and cloud. Likewise with the things revealed in certain mystical and divine insights concerning truth: the same variation is experienced by the person who serves God, with the apperception of the assistance of divine power which suddenly attaches itself to the intellect—or it may be the apperception of the opposite, where the intention is that he should receive awareness of the weakness of human nature, and realize what his own nature is, and how weak, feeble, stupid and childish it is …

Periods of abandonment and spiritual decay are necessary for a person that he may perceive his helplessness and dependence upon God. Abandonment (meštabqanuta) is not God withdrawing from a person: it is a subjective sense of God's absence; this person is not really forgotten by God but God leaves him alone with the reality that surrounds him. Antony the Great was left alone for many days to struggle against the demons; when he was completely exhausted, God appeared to him as a ray of light. 'Where were you?' Antony asked, 'why didn't you come in the beginning, to stop my sufferings?' The voice of God answered him: 'I was here, Antony, but I waited to see you struggle'. It is God's will that, through the experience of abandonment, a person may gain his own victory and become worthy of God.

Since the fall of Adam, abandonment has been an experience common to the whole of humanity—both believers and unbelievers. For a believer, however, it is an experience of the temporary absence of God, and gives place to an intense feeling of presence; for an atheist it is an experience of constant and irreparable absence. An atheist considers the absence of God the norm; a believer endures the feeling of absence as very strong and intensely painful suffering. He cannot cope with the absence of God. Even though in his mind he knows that God has not forgotten him, his soul and heart thirst for conscious experience of God's presence. The life in God is accompanied with the feeling of God's presence, and when this feeling is lost, a believer cannot find calm until it returns.

Abandonment is the critical stage of one's spiritual development wherein one's attitude to God is tested in a very profound way. For any Christian, the experience of abandonment has only two possible outcomes—either growth of faith and drawing nearer to God, or a 'shipwreck' of faith and loss of God. Thus Isaac cautions against cursing God during periods of abandonment and against yielding to a temptation which may lead to a loss of faith. When someone is deprived of grace, Isaac says, trust in God and a right way of thinking about God's providence are abandoned; the person can come to the 'conclusion that God no longer exists for him'. Yet instead of being angry at God, a person should remind himself of God's good providence and calm himself down:

Draw near a little to God in your trials, O fellow human being, by means of your mental disposition. Are you really aware against whom you are thundering away? You would immediately find relief if you have the wisdom to remember the hidden providence of this very same God.

This feeling of abandonment occurs for various reasons. Sometimes the reason is a person's own negligence and shortness of patience, as well as pride. In this case abandonment appears as faint-heartedness and despondency, which is a hell on earth:

When it is God's pleasure to subject a man to even greater afflictions, he permits him to fall into the hands of faint-heartedness. This begets in him a mighty force of despondency, wherein he feels his soul being suffocated. This is a foretaste of gehenna. From this, there is unleashed upon him the spirit of aberration—from which ten thousand trials gush forth; confusion; wrath; blasphemy; protesting and bewailing one's lot; perverted thoughts; wandering from place to place; and the like. And if you should ask what the cause of these things is, I answer that it is you yourself, for the reason that you have not taken pains to find the remedy for them. The remedy for them is ... humility of heart.

The feeling of abandonment may also overwhelm someone for reasons which do not depend on him at all. In particular, periods of abandonment, depression, darkening, and despair envelop ascetics who live in stillness. In this case the reason is the ineffable providence of God:

Let us not be troubled when we are found in darkness, especially if the cause of it is not in us. But reckon this as the work of God's providence for a reason which he alone knows. At times our soul is suffocated and is, as it were, amid the waves; and whether a man reads the Scriptures, or performs his liturgy, or approaches anything whatever, he receives darkness upon darkness. He leaves off prayer and cannot even draw nigh to it. He is wholly unable to believe that a change will occur and that he will be at peace. This hour is full of despair and fear; hope in God and the consolation of faith are utterly effaced from his soul, and she is wholly and entirely filled with doubt and fear.

However, Isaac continues, God does not leave the soul in this state for very long. After the period of despair, a change for the better should take place:

Those who are tried by the billows of this hour know from experience the change that follows upon its completion. God does not leave the soul in these things an entire day, for otherwise she would perish, being estranged from the Christian hope; but he speedily provides her with an escape.

What should an ascetic do during periods of abandonment and darkness? A normal piece of advice would be to pray until it passes: 'During periods of these temptations, when someone is darkened, he ought to fall on his face in prayer, and not rise up until power come to him from heaven and a light which will support his heart in a faith that has no doubts'.

Another recommendation is to remember one's initial zeal and early years of the ascetical life:

At the time of your defeat ... ponder in your heart on the former time of your diligence, and how you used to concern yourself even over the most minute matters, and the valiant struggle which you displayed, and how you were stirred up with zeal against those who would hinder you in your progress. ... For thus, with such and so many recollections, your soul is wakened as if from deep sleep and is clad with the flame of zeal. ... She rises up out of her sunken state as if from the dead, she is raised on high, and she returns to her ancient estate.

Isaac also recommends occupying oneself with the reading of patristic writings:

Whenever it happens to you ... that your soul is enshrouded by thick darkness from within and, as with the sun's rays when they are hidden from the earth in the midst of clouds, for a brief time she is deprived of spiritual comfort and the light of grace on account of the cloud of passions that overshadows her; and further, when the joy-producing power in your soul is curtailed for a little, and your mind is overshadowed by an unwonted mist: then do not be troubled in your mind, do not give way to despondency. But be patient, be engaged in reading the books of the Doctors of the Church, compel yourself in prayer, and expect to receive help. Then straightway help will come unawares.

'Scriptural reading' (qeryana—a syriac term referring to both the Bible and the Church Fathers) casts away despondency and darkness from the soul:

I myself have had many experiences of these things, and what I have discovered is along the lines of what I have indicated here as a reminder, out of brotherly love, since many, I think, are benefited by these experiences, and they make progress as they come to realize that in half the cases of a sense of heaviness during stillness, this is dissolved by some form of scriptural reading; in some cases, by means of the discernment they taste as a result of the illumination provided by the wisdom that lies in the words.

The sense of abandonment and despondency may, however, be so severe that a person cannot find the strength in himself either to read the Scriptures or to pray. In these circumstances, Isaac offers the following recommendation:

If you do not have the strength to master yourself and to fall upon your face in prayer, then wrap your head in your cloak and sleep until this hour of darkness pass from you, but do not leave your dwelling. This trial befalls those especially who desire to pass their life in the discipline of the mind, and who throughout their journey seek the consolation of faith. For this reason their greatest pain and travail is the dark hour when their mind wavers with doubt. And blasphemy follows hard upon this. Sometimes the man is seized by doubts in the resurrection, and by other things whereof we have no need to speak. Many times we have experienced all these things, and we have written of this struggle for the comfort of many. ... Blessed is he who patiently endures these things within the doors of his cell! Afterwards, as Fathers say, he will attain to a magnificent and powerful dwelling.

At the same time, Isaac continues, it is impossible to liberate oneself completely from periods of darkening and abandonment, and to reach perfect rest in this earthly life. A variation of periods of darkness and light is characteristic of the life of the solitary until the very hour of his death: 'Sometimes trial, sometimes consolation. A man continues in these things until his departure. In this life we should not expect to receive perfect freedom from this struggle, nor to receive perfect consolation'.

These periods of darkness and abandonment Isaac compares to winter; natural life almost completely ceases, but the seeds lie deep in the earth, waiting for spring, when they put out new shoots. One should not fall into despair but rather wait patiently until the afflictions, despondency, and abandonment that one has endured bring their fruits:

How blessed is the person who, out of hope for God's grace, has endured the dejectedness which is a hidden trial of the mind's virtue and growth. It is like the gloom of winter, which nevertheless causes the hidden seed to grow as it disintegrates under the ground in the harsh changes of blustery weather. With the same expectation of fruit in the end, by placing this expectation over an extended period of time, a person will push dejectedness away from himself. ... Thus he should await at a distance, not considering them to be close at hand. For when he has not received consolation at his labours in the short term, he may end up in despair, like the hired labourer who has been cheated of the wage for which he has worked.

As suddenly and unexpectedly as it began, the winter cold ends and the spring of the soul burgeons:

God permits coldness and heaviness to come upon a man to train and test him. But if he zealously rouses himself and compels himself a little to shake off these things, then grace will immediately draw near him, as it did formerly, and a different power will come upon him, bearing hidden within it all that is good and every manner of succour.

He will marvel with great astonishment, bringing to mind both the former heaviness and the lightness and strength which has now overtaken him and considering both the difference between them and his present state, and how such a great change has so suddenly found him. Thenceforth he will be wise, and if again such heaviness should come upon him, he will know about it by his former experience.

Isaac describes in bright colours the state of spiritual enlightenment and exultation which follows the period of darkness:

There are times when a person sits in a stillness … and there is no entry or exit for him. But after much converse with the Scriptures, continuous supplication and thanksgiving at his feeble state, with his gaze extended unceasingly towards God's grace after great dejection in the stillness, and little by little from that starting point some spaciousness of heart is born, and a germination takes place which gives birth to joy from within, even though that joy has no origin within that person himself, by some kind of initiating process of thought. He is aware that his heart is rejoicing, but he does not know the reason why. For a kind of exultation takes hold of the soul; in its enjoyment everything that exists and is seen is disregarded, and the mind sees, through its power, whence comes the foundation of that rapture of thought—but why it occurs he does not comprehend. He sees that the mind is raised up from its association with everything else, is lifted up and finds itself above the world in its upsurge … but does not discern any extension of intellect at this leaping of the heart or at the drawing out of the mind during its vexation.

In this way an ascetic acquires experience from enduring temptations and ascends from one step to another on the ladder leading to God. Trials and temptations, according to Isaac, are necessary for everyone on the way to God. Of these trials the most painful is that of abandonment, the experience of 'tasting gehenna'. One falls into darkness and despondency, loses hope and the consolation of faith. One should not despair but rather think of the providence of God, who 'will, with the temptation, also make a way to escape', as well as remain humble and pray as zealously as is possible. Temptation will assuredly be replaced by a period of closeness of God, and the feeling of abandonment will change to a sense of God's presence.

CHAPTER IV

HUMILITY

Humility is the raiment of the Godhead.
I/77 (381) = PR 82 (575)

Blessed is he who humbles himself in all things, for he will be exalted in all. For a man who for God's sake humbles himself and thinks meanly of himself is glorified by God. The man who hungers and thirsts for God's sake, God will make drunk with that wine whose inebriation never passes from those who drink it. And he who goes naked for God's sake is clad by Him in a robe of incorruption and glory. And he who becomes poor for His sake is consoled with His true riches.

I/5 (50–51) = PR 5 (77)

ONE OF ISAAC'S CONSTANT THEMES, to which he returns many times, is humility. Several homilies from Parts I and II are entirely dedicated to this subject. In this chapter we shall look at Isaac's teaching on humility as assimilation to God and at internal and external signs of true humility.

1. HUMILITY AS ASSIMILATION TO GOD

To speak of humility (mukkaka or makkikuta) meant to Isaac to speak of God, for God in his vision is primarily the One who is 'meek and lowly in heart'. God's humility was revealed to the world in the Incarnation of the Word. In the Old Testament, God remained invisible to and unattainable by everyone approaching him. But when he clothed himself in humility and hid his glory under human flesh, he became both visible and attainable:

Humility is the raiment of the Godhead. The Word who became human clothed himself in it, and he spoke to us in our body. Everyone who has been clothed with humility has truly been made like unto Him who came down from his own exaltedness and hid the splendour of his majesty and concealed his glory with humility, lest creation be utterly consumed by the contemplation of him.

Every Christian is called to imitate Christ in humility. In acquiring humility, a person becomes like the Lord and clothes himself in Christ:

Wherefore every man has put on Christ when he is clothed with the raiment wherein the Creator was seen through the body that he put on. For the likeness in which he was seen by his own creation and in which he kept company with it, he willed to put on in his inner man, and to be seen therein by his fellow-servants.

Humility together with rightly directed labours 'makes man god on earth'.

Adoption by and assimilation to God happen, according to Isaac, not so much through various ascetical labours as through acquiring humility. The labours without humility bring no profit, whereas humility without any ascetic exercises is sufficient for adoption by God:

Humility, even without works, gains forgiveness for many offenses; but without her, works are of no profit to us and instead prepare for us great evils. Therefore, through humility, as I said, find forgiveness for your iniquitous deeds. What salt is for any food, humility is for every virtue, and she can mightily obliterate many sins. ... And if she becomes ours, she will make us sons of God, and even without good works she will present us to God. For without humility all our works are vain—every virtue and every righteous labour.

Accordingly, a person should not wait until he gains humility for the fruits of his spiritual labour, even if he makes many ascetical efforts to reach his aim: 'If you practice an excellent virtue without perceiving the taste of its aid, do not marvel; for until a man becomes humble, he will not receive a reward for his labour. Recompense is given, not for labour, but for humility.'

In putting on humility, a person becomes so godlike that he is loved by eveyone around him and is regarded as a god on earth. Humility helps restore the reign of love amongst people.

No one ever hates or wounds with words or despises someone who is humble, for because his Master loves him, he is loved by all. He loves all and is loved by all. All men cherish him, and in every place he approaches they see him as an angel of light and mark him out with honour. And though the wise man and the teacher discourse, they are silenced, that they may yield their place to the humble man to speak. The eyes of all give heed to his mouth, and to whatever word issues from it. And every man waits on his words, even as on the words of God. ... He is announced as a god by all men, even though he be inexpert in his speech, and despicable and vile in his appearance.

Assimilation to God through humility brings a human being back to the primordial sinless state and to that harmony between him and the universe which was lost as a result of the fall. Not only people, but also animals and the elements, obey the humble, as they obeyed Adam in paradise. Even the demons become his slaves:

The humble man approaches ravening beasts, and when their gaze rests upon him, their wildness is tamed. They come up to him as to their master, wag their heads and tails and lick his hands and feet, for they smell coming from him that same scent that exhaled from Adam before the fall, when they were gathered before him and he gave them names in Paradise.... . Even the demons with their fierceness, their hostility, and all their boastful thinking, become like dust as soon as they come before him. All their wickedness becomes folly, and their stratagems are undone, and their wiles and pernicious cunning are rendered powerless.

Humility, by Isaac's definition, is a certain mysterious power which is acquired by the saints when they reach the state of perfection. This power was granted to the Apostles on the day of Pentecost, when they should receive the power from on high after Jesus had commanded them not to depart from Jerusalem.

The humble are accounted worthy of receiving in themselves the Spirit of revelations who teaches mysteries. On this account it has been said by certain holy men that humility perfects the soul through divine visions. ... Blessed is he that has gained it, because at every moment he kisses and embraces the bosom of Jesus!

If humility is a supernatural gift of God, not everyone who is by nature gentle, quiet, prudent, or meek can be regarded as humble. There is a difference between natural and supernatural humility, as Isaac discusses in Chapter XVIII of Part II. There he claims that natural humility cannot be a substitute for that humility which is born in a Christian by deep repentance and the memory of God's greatness and Christ's humility:

Humility of heart can occur in someone for two reasons: either as a result of a precise knowledge of one's sins; or as a result of recollecting the lowliness of our Lord— or rather, as a result of recollecting the greatness of God and the extent to which the greatness of the Lord lowered itself in order to speak to and instruct us human beings in various ways—so abasing himself that he even took a body from humanity. How much did our Lord's body endure, what did it have to go through, how despised did he appear to the world, while all the time he possessed ineffable glory on high with God the Father, with the angels trembling at the sight of him as the glory of his countenance blazed among their ranks! In our case, he appeared in such lowliness that human beings could, because of the ordinariness of his appearance, seize hold of him as he spoke with them and hang him on the wood of the cross.

Natural humility has little in common with this supernatural humility:

Do not adduce for me as an example those who are humble by nature, saying that there are many such people whose very nature testifies that they are humble. … [These people] do not possess this discerning lowliness which consists in lowly thoughts, discerning and painstaking reflection, the insignificance in which a person regards himself, his heart broken, and the flow of tears stemming from suffering of mind and discernment of the will. If you choose, ask them. You will find that they have none of these, no meditation that causes them real suffering, no real concern over their consciences. They do not meditate and recollect the lowliness of our Lord; they are not pierced by the sharp pain that comes from a knowledge of their sins; there is no burning fervour which enflames their hearts at the recollection of the good things that are to come; they have none of the other advantageous thoughts that are normally stirred up in the heart as a result of the mind's wakefulness.

If one is to include in the ranks of the humble all those who are meek and gentle by nature, then one must number eunuchs among virgins and the consecrated, even though it was only nature, and not their own will, that kept them from marriage. 'It is exactly the same with those who are mild and humble by nature: it is nature which has moderated their impulses, and not strength of will. These people neither taste nor are they in the slightest aware of the sweetness of the charisms and consolations of which those who are humble for our Lord's sake taste'.

2. HUMILITY AS AN INNER QUALITY

Humility is primarily an inner quality. It consists in trust in God, absence of hope in one's self, the sense of one's own unworthiness and defenselessness, the presence of the Holy Spirit hidden in the depths of the heart. At the same time humility reveals itself outwardly; it is expressed in lowly appearance and poor clothing, in lack of verbosity and obtrusiveness, in giving honour to others, in trying to avoid privileges, in enduring offenses and afflictions. The inward and outward aspects of humility are inseparably linked. Outward humility is false unless a person humbles himself before God in his heart, and inward humility cannot be true if it in no way reveals itself outwardly.

By this understanding, there are both inward and outward signs of humility. Drawing a boundary line between them is difficult, as we see in the following passage:

Humility is accompanied by modesty and self-collectedness: that is, chastity of the senses; a moderated voice; mean speech; self-belittlement; poor raiment; a gait that is not pompous; a gaze directed toward the earth; superabundant mercy; easily flowing tears; a solitary soul; a contrite heart; imperturbability to anger; undistracted senses; few possessions; moderation in every need; endurance; patience; fearlessness; manliness of heart born of a hatred for this temporal life; patient endurance of trials; deliberations that are ponderous, not light; extinction of thoughts; guarding of mysteries; chastity; modesty; reverence; and above all, continually to be still and always to claim ignorance.

In this catalogue of the marks of humility both inward and outward qualities are listed without any specific classification.

If we were to classify the signs of humility and to speak first of inner signs, the first of them would be a deep sense of God's presence, out of which humility is born. A person cannot be humble by himself, by means of his own efforts and external activities: he humbles himself when, in encountering God, he perceives God's greatness and his own nothingness. After such an encounter a person comes to God in deep silence of heart, not even considering himself worthy to utter the words of prayer in the presence of Him who is above all words. This silent, humble prayer leads a person to mystical depths of divine contemplation:

I should marvel greatly if there were any truly humble man who would venture to supplicate God when he draws nigh to prayer, or to ask to be accounted worthy of prayer, or to make entreaty for any other thing, or who would know what to pray. For the humble man keeps a reign of silence over all his deliberations, and simply awaits mercy and whatever decree should come forth concerning him from the countenance of God's worshipful majesty. ... When he bows his head to the earth, and contemplation within his heart is raised to the sublime gate leading to the Holy of Holies wherein is He whose dwelling place is darkness which dims the eyes of the Seraphim and whose brilliance awes the legions of their choirs and sheds silence upon all their orders. ... Then he dares only to speak and pray thus, 'May it be unto me according to thy will, O Lord'.

Another inner sign of humility is death to the world: 'The man who has acquired humility in his heart is dead to this world'. Revulsion for this world is a sign of humility which comes from spiritual wisdom:

Question: Whence does a man perceive that he has received wisdom from the Spirit?

Answer: From the knowledge that teaches him the ways of humility in his hidden depths and in his senses, and reveals to him in his intellect how humility is received.

Question: Whence does a man perceive that he has attained to humility?

Answer: From the fact that he regards it as odious to please the world either in his association with it or by word, and the glory of this world is an abomination in his eye.

The awakening of the voice of conscience in a person is yet another inner sign of humility. It teaches him not to accuse God or his neighbour in anything, not to lay the blame on the occurrences of life or to justify himself. The person who listens to the voice of his conscience will attain spiritual stillness and reconciliation with God:

The continual reprimands of the conscience are a sign of humility. The lack of these in any undertaking is a sign of hardness in heart: it is an indication that a person is in the habit of justifying himself, of blaming his neighbour instead—or, even worse, of blaming the wise provision of God. Conversely, a person cannot leave the boundaries of humility unless he first sees himself as being without blame, blaming instead the events and occasions which have been provided for him by God. For when, as a result of a strict conscience, he observes himself subject to events, then a person will recognize that his condition is one of a profound degree of humility. This will be recognized by the fact that he is in a state of peace and tranquillity at all that happens to him; for he proves to be imperturbed - and this is the restful state which belongs to humility, and is the fruit of maturity. Whoever has entered this will find that in every temptation his feeling of rest will be greater than his feeling of vexation.

Inner stillness is one of the characteristic signs of humility. It manifests itself in the absence of fear amid life's circumstances, in confidence in the divine providence which protects one from every evil:

A humble man is never rushed, hasty, or agitated, never has any hot or volatile thoughts, but at all times remains calm. Even if heaven were to fall and cleave to the earth, the humble man would not be dismayed. Not every quiet man is humble, but every humble man is quiet,... for the humble man is always at rest, because there is nothing which can agitate or shake his mind. Just as no one can frighten a mountain, so the mind of a humble man cannot be frightened.

The humble person does not fear accidental occurrences, for it is only God whom he fears: the fear of God drives any other fear away from his heart. The notion of the fear of God presupposes an attitude to him that is characterized by a religious trepidation before him, an effort not to offend him by any sinful deed or thought. Humility, according to Isaac, is born of the fear of God. Humility involves contrition of heart, the fear of God, and spiritual joy:

There is a humility that comes from the fear of God, and a humility that comes from the fervent love of God. One man is humbled because of his fear of God; another is humbled because of his joy. The man humbled by fear of God is possessed of modesty in his members, a right ordering of his senses, and a heart contrite at all times. But the man humbled because of joy is possessed of great exuberance and an open and insuppressible heart.

Isaac compares humility with infancy: the humble for the sake of God are like infants in their simplicity and innocence. The exhortation to become like children is part of the message of Jesus: 'Except ye be converted, and become as little children, ye shall not enter into the kingdom of heaven'. The exegetes of the antiochene school interpreted this text as an indication that a Christian should be humble and simple-hearted. Developing this theme, Isaac points out that the defenselessness of small children forces God to take particular care of them. The humble should be similarly defenseless:

It has been said, 'The Lord preserveth the infants'. An infant goes up to a snake and clasps it by the neck, and it does him no harm. An infant goes naked all winter long, when everyone else is dressed and covered up, and the cold steals over all his limbs unfelt. He sits naked on a day of cold, ice, and frost and suffers nothing because the body of his innocence is swaddled with another, invisible, garment woven of that hidden providence which protects his tender limbs, lest harm from any source come near him. ... 'The Lord preserveth the infants'. And not only those who are tiny in body, but also those who, being wise in the world, abandon their knowledge,... applying themselves entirely to that other, all-sufficing wisdom, and becoming like babes in their own free will... .

Therefore, the humble person is preserved under the special protection of God's providence: it covers him like clothing, protecting him from every danger from outside. In other words, the humble enters into a special relationship with God: renouncing natural means of self-defense, he puts his whole trust in God, who 'preserveth the infants'.

In human weakness, the strength of God is made perfect, as Saint Paul claimed. When a person becomes aware of his own weakness and calls on God to come to his aid, he will undoubtedly receive this aid. Between humility and prayer there is an unbroken link:

Blessed is the man who knows his own weakness, for this knowledge becomes for him the foundation, the root, and the beginning of all goodness. ... When a man knows that he is in need of divine help, he offers up many prayers. And by as much as he multiplies them is his heart humbled, for there is no man who will not be humbled when he is offering supplication and entreaty. 'A heart that is broken and humbled, God will not despise'.

One should therefore pray to reach the state of humility, because it is impossible to attain to it using only human means. As Isaac says:

What is impossible with humanity can very well happen with God. Instead of making your prayer on the topic of this thing or another, or concerning that matter or another, abandon all these and rely on a single prayer, saying, 'O God, grant me humility so that I may be freed from the lash, so that with humility I may draw near even to those delights of the mind of which I am unaware—however much I may desire to know them—before I acquire this humility'. And God will then give you the gift of his Spirit, a gift whose greatness you are not capable of speaking about or conceiving, for by it you will be made humble in a hidden way. ... My brother, believe that humility is a power which cannot be described by the tongue, nor can it be acquired by human power; rather, it is given in prayer to whomsoever it may be given, and it is received amidst vigils consisting of supplication and fervent entreaties.

3. EXTERNAL SIGNS OF HUMILITY

When we turn to external signs of humility, we must speak in particular of the absence of any interest in earthly distractions and pleasures, of striving to avoid worldly cares and luxury. A person who possesses a great deal of money, who is preoccupied with labour, or who takes part in social activity, is bound hand and foot by the ties of this world. On the other hand, the person who avoids all of these entanglements, preserves godlike freedom:

A humble man is never pleased to see gatherings, confused crowds, tumult, shouts and cries, opulence, adornment, and luxury, the cause of insobriety; nor does he take pleasure in conversations, assemblies, noise, and the scattering of the senses; but above all else he chooses to be by himself and to collect himself within himself—being alone in stillness, separated from all creation, and taking heed of himself in a silent place. Insignificance, absence of possessions, want, and poverty are in every way beloved by him. He is not engaged in manifold and fluctuating affairs, but at all times he desires to be unoccupied and free of the cares and the confusion of the things of this world, that he may keep his thoughts from going outside himself. ... For all these reasons a humble man unceasingly protects himself from many affairs, and thus at all times he is found tranquil, gentle, peaceful, modest, and reverent.

This attitude towards life, the choice not to be involved in worldly activities and to feel oneself as a guest in human society, greek ascetical writers call xeniteia, which means 'exile' or, literally, 'living as a stranger' (from xenos, 'stranger'). The syriac rendering of this term is aksenayuta (from aksenaya, 'stranger'). An ascetic should be 'living as a stranger', according to Isaac, in every place and at all times: 'Consider yourself a stranger all the days of your life, wherever you may be ...' In the ascetical tradition, xeniteia consists, not in a nomadic existence, but in withdrawal from the world and worldly entertainment, in a sense of the shortness and fragility of this life, the renunciation of the earthly for the sake of the heavenly. This xeniteia leads to humility:

How can man acquire humility? ... By an unceasing remembrance of transgressions; by the anticipation of approaching death; by inexpensive clothing; by always preferring the last place; by always running to do the tasks that are the most insignificant and distasteful; by not being disobedient; by unceasing silence; by a dislike of gatherings; by desiring to be unknown and of no account; by never holding to one sort of work exclusively; by shunning conversation with numerous persons; by abhorrence of material gain; and, after these things, by raising the mind above the reproach and accusation of every man and above zealotry; by not being a man whose hand is against everyone and against whom is everyone's hand, but rather someone who remains alone, occupied with his own affairs; by having no concern for anyone in the world save himself. In brief, exile, poverty, and a solitary life give birth to humility and cleanse the heart.

Another external manifestation of humility is the uncomplaining endurance of all sorts of humiliations:

Suffer contempt and humiliation with good will, that you may have boldness before God. The man who knowingly endures all manner of harsh words, without having previously wronged his chider, at that moment places a crown of thorns on his head, and he is blessed, for he is crowned with an imperishable crown in a time which he knows not.

Isaac considers the unmurmuring endurance of offenses and accusations as the highest virtue:

Someone who is able to suffer wrong with joy, though having at hand the means to rebuff it, has consciously received from God the consolation of his faith. The man who endures accusations against himself with humility has arrived at perfection, and he is marveled at by the holy angels, for there is no other virtue so great and so hard to achieve.

Humility is also manifested in a person's striving to be humiliated by other people:

As grace accompanies humility, so painful incidents accompany pride. The eyes of the

Lord are upon the humble to make them glad; but the face of the Lord is against the proud to make them humble. Humility always receives mercy from God; but hardness of heart and littleness of faith contend with fearful encounters. … In all respects belittle yourself before all men, and you will be raised above the princes of this age. Anticipate every person with your greeting and your bow, and you will be more highly prized than those who bring the gold of Ophir as a gift. Be contemptible in your own eyes, and you will see the glory of God within yourself. For where humility burgeons, there God's glory wells forth. If you strive to be slighted openly by all men, God will cause you to be glorified. If you have humility in your heart, then in your heart God will show you his glory. Be disdained in your greatness, and not great in your insignificance. Endeavour to be despised, and you will be filled with the honour of God. Seek not to be honoured while within you are full of wounds. Deprecate honour, that you may be honoured; and do not love it, that you may be dishonoured.

True humility, according to Isaac, reveals itself in honouring one's neighbour more even than he deserves. The humble person will treat everyone he encounters with respect, honour and love:

When you meet your fellow man, constrain yourself to pay him more honour than is his due. Kiss his hands and feet; often take his hand with deep respect, put them over your eyes, and praise him for what he does not even possess. And when he parts from you, say every good thing about him, and whatever it may be that commands respect. For by these and similar acts, you draw him to good … and you sow the seeds of virtue in him.

Though Isaac speaks here of 'constraining' oneself to paying honour to a fellow human being, he does not mean having an artificially affectionate attitude: rather, this attitude should be a natural consequence of a true love of one's neighbour, deepest respect for him, and a sense of one's own unworthiness before him.

An extreme outward manifestation of inner humility is 'holy folly', a fairly widespread phenomenon in the Orthodox East at the time of Isaac the Syrian. To be 'a holy fool' means deliberately to take upon oneself the appearance of a fool or to commit certain reprehensible actions in order to be condemned and despised by other people. Holy folly was exercised by ascetics who became renowned for their virtuous and saintly life: devoid of an opportunity to endure offenses and humiliation, they put on a mask of madness in order to recover this opportunity. 'If a man', Isaac writes, 'does not despise honours and dishonours, and if, for the sake of stillness, he does not patiently endure reproach, mocking, injury, and even blows and become a laughing-stock, considered by all who see him to be a fool and a half-wit, he cannot persevere in the good things of stillness'.

Isaac cites as an example ancient saints who took upon themselves the mask of folly for the sake of avoiding human glory, and who, in order to be humiliated, even confessed sins that they did not commit:

A man who is truly humble is not troubled when he is wronged and he says nothing to justify himself against the injustice, but he accepts slander as truth; he does not attempt to persuade men that he is calumniated, but he begs forgiveness. Some have voluntarily drawn upon themselves the repute of being licentious, when they are not; others have endured the charge of adultery, being far from it, and have proclaimed by their tears that they bear the fruit of sins they have not committed, and have wept, asking their offenders' forgiveness for the iniquity they have not perpetrated; all the while their souls are crowned with all purity and chastity. Others, lest they be glorified for the virtuous state they have hidden within them, have pretended to be lunatics, while in truth they were so permeated with divine salt and so securely fixed in serenity, because of their uttermost perfection, that they had holy angels as heralds of their deeds of valour.

Isaac shares with us his own personal memoirs of conversations on the theme of holy folly with famous ascetics of the time of his monastic youth. He tells us about how he once went to 'a certain elder, an excellent and virtuous man' and said to him: 'Father, the thought comes to me to go early to the portico of the church on Sunday and to sit down there and eat, so that everyone who enters or departs would see and scorn me'. In answer to this the elder replied:

It is written that every man who causes scandal for those of the world shall not see light. No one knows you in this region, nor does anyone know what your fame is, and so they will say, 'The monks eat from the morning hours'. ... The fathers of old did such things because of the many miracles which they worked and the honour and great name they possessed among men. They did this, that they might be dishonoured, to hide the glory of their way of life, and to drive away from themselves the causes of pride. But what necessity obliges you to do such a thing? Do you know that every discipline has its rule and time? Your way of life is not singular, nor your name famous, for your discipline is [simply] that of the brethren; this thing would not be profitable to you and you would harm the others. Furthermore, such things are done by way of dispensation and are not beneficial for every man, but only the great and perfect'.

In this way the elder tried to temper the young ascetic's fervour and prevent him from committing acts which were blameworthy from the point of view of monastic ethics, even if the aim of all this was obtaining humility.

———————————

CHAPTER V

TEARS

It is you who grant repentance and a sorrowing heart to the sinner who repents; in this way you ease his heart of the weight of sin that is laid upon it, thanks to the comfort which comes from sorrowing and from the gift of tears.

II/5,3.

SAINT ISAAC'S TEACHING ON TEARS is closely connected with the theme of repentance. As we shall see, however, he speaks not only of weeping in repentance for sins but also of the tears of compunction that well up in a person at his encounter with God. In this chapter we shall discuss Isaac's teaching on repentance and then his notion of the two kinds of tears: bitter tears of repentance; and sweet tears of compunction.

1. REPENTANCE

Following Aphrahat and John the Solitary, Isaac speaks of repentance as a medicine invented by God for the constant renewal and healing of a person:

Because God, with that compassionate knowledge of his, knew that if genuine righteousness were required of human beings, then only one in ten thousand would be found who could enter the kingdom of heaven, he accordingly provided them instead with a medicine suitable for everyone, namely repentance, so that on every day and at every moment there would be available to them an opportunity easily to be put in the right by means of the strength of this medicine: through compunction they would be able at any time to wash away from themselves every stain they might incur; they would be able to be renewed each day through repentance. How great are the means which our compassionate Maker has, in the wisdom of his divinity, provided us for the sake of our everlasting life (ḥayye), for it is his wish that we should be renewed each day and begin again with a virtuous change of will and a renewal of mind.

Repentance is the constant spiritual state of an ascetic; it should be forever present in the heart: 'At every moment we should know that we stand in need of repentance throughout the twenty-four hours of the night and day'. Repentance should not be limited to a certain period in a person's life nor considered the lot of a certain category of people. Repentance is universal:

If we are all sinners and no man is above sin's temptations, it is certainly true that no virtue is more pre-eminent than repentance. (For a man can never complete the work of repentance. It is always suitable to every sinner and righteous man who wishes to gain salvation. There is no limit to perfection, for even the perfection of the perfect is truly without completion. And for this very reason repentance is bounded neither by periods of time nor by works until a man's death).

Isaac defines repentance as the 'abandoning of former deeds and grieving for them'. Using another definition, he writes: 'the meaning of the word repentance (tyabuta) ... is this: continual and mournful supplication which by means of prayer filled with compunction draws nigh to God in order to seek forgiveness of past offenses, and entreaty for preservation from future'. In the latter definition we can distinguish three points. First, repentance is prayer to God, it is standing before God and not merely thinking about past sins within oneself. Secondly, it is the renunciation of one's sinful past and regret for it. Thirdly, it is looking forward towards the future, and choosing to preserve oneself from sin. Repentance is, therefore, a synthetic act: it includes standing before God, regretting past sins and willing to avoid them in the future.

Repentance can be compared with a ship by which a person crosses the sea that separates him from the noetic paradise. The pilot of this ship is the fear of God, and the goal of the journey and its haven is divine love. Into this haven enter all who are 'afflicted and heavy laden' in repentance. 'Rig together my impulses for the ship of repentance', Isaac prays, 'so that in it I may exult as I travel over the world's sea until I reach the haven of your hope.'

It is traditional in patristic literature to present repentance as a second baptism, and Isaac develops this same theme. According to him, God did not wish that human beings, who abused their freedom, should be deprived of the blessed state that had been prepared for them, and thus God 'in his mercifulness devised a second gift, which is repentance, so that by it the soul's life might acquire renewal every day and thereby every time be put aright'. Repentance is the renewal of the grace of baptism that was lost after humanity's fall:

Repentance is given to man as grace after grace, for repentance is a second regeneration by God. That of which we have received an earnest by baptism, we receive as a gift by means of repentance. Repentance is the door of mercy, opened to those who seek it. By this door we enter into the mercy of God, and apart from this entrance we shall not find mercy. … Repentance is the second grace …

Through repentance a person receives back that knowledge which was given to him as a pledge in baptism.

Repentance arises in a person through the activity of divine grace in the soul. It begins when God bestows on us a consciousness of our own sins. This consciousness penetrates into our thoughts as God sees to it that we suffer multifarious trials. Perceiving one's own sins, Isaac claims, is more important than performing miracles or having supernatural mystical visions, for with this awareness the way of repentance begins. And repentance itself is higher than many other virtues:

The man who is conscious of his sins is greater than someone who profits the whole world by the sight of his countenance. The man who sighs over his soul for but one hour is greater than someone who raises the dead by his prayer while dwelling amid many men. The man who is deemed worthy to see himself is greater than someone who is deemed worthy to see the angels, for the latter has communion through his bodily eyes, but the former through the eyes of his soul. The man who follows Christ in solitary mourning is greater than someone who praises God in the congregation of men.

Repentance is an integral act involving both the heart and the intellect of a person. Isaac speaks of the 'grief of the heart' and 'sorrow of mind' as attributes of repentance. 'A broken and a contrite heart', of which the Psalms speak, is acquired by a person in the process of repenting and realizing his own sins and this is at the same time deliverance from the burden of these sins: 'It is You who grant repentance and a sorrowing heart to the sinner who repents; in this way You ease his heart of the weight of sin that is laid upon it, thanks to the comfort which comes from sorrowing and from the gift of tears'.

Forgiveness of sins, the fruit of repentance, immediately follows repentance, and the reason for this is God's immeasurable love for humankind, the love which impelled the Son of God not only to forgive all sinners but also to become human for the deliverance of human persons from sins: 'Seeing that his face is set all the time towards forgiveness,... he pours over us his immense grace that, like the ocean, knows no measure. To anyone who shows just a little suffering and the will to compunction for what has occurred, to such a person immediately, at once, without any delay, he will grant forgiveness of their sins'.

For this reason a Christian should never doubt that his sins, even grave sins, are forgiven by God as soon as he repents. Confidence in forgiveness derives from faith in God's mercy, which surpasses God's justice, in divine providence, and especially in the Incarnation of God the Word which is a pledge of reconciliation between God and the humanity:

Who, on seeing and hearing these things, will be stirred by that recollection of his sins which will raise doubt in his mind: 'Will God, if I ask him, forgive me these things by which I am pained and by whose memory I am tormented, things by which, though I abhor them, I go on backsliding? Yet after they have taken place the pain they give me is even greater than that of a scorpion's sting. Though I abhor them, I am still in the middle of them, and when I repent of them with suffering I wretchedly return to them again.' This is how many God-fearing people think, people who foster virtue and are pricked with the suffering of compunction, who mourn over their sin; yet human prosperity compels them to bear with the backsliding which results from it. They live between sin and repentance all the time. Let us not be in doubt, O fellow humanity, concerning the hope of our salvation, seeing that he who bore sufferings for our sakes is very concerned about our salvation; his mercifulness is far more extensive than we can conceive, his grace is greater than what we ask for. For the right hand of our Lord is stretched out night and day, while he is on the look out to support, comfort, and encourage everyone—especially to see if he can find any who endure even just a little suffering and grief so that their sins may be forgiven—people who are grieved over the small portion of their righteousness ...

Through the act of repentance, reconciliation between God and a human person takes place. A person is required to repent the sins he has committed, to make a decisive act of will to preserve himself from them in the future, to maintain a prayerful attitude before God, and to ask for forgiveness. The forgiveness which comes from God, reconciles the penitent with God and lets him participate in divine love.

2. BITTER AND SWEET TEARS

The gift of tears is a characteristic theme of syriac ascetical literature, and an integral part of Isaac the Syrian's monastic spirituality.

In Syriac, the word abila, 'a mourner', was used to designate a monk. According to syrian tradition, a monk is primarily someone who mourns for himself, for others, for the whole world. 'A mourner (abila) is he who passes all the days of his life in hunger and thirst for the sake of his hope and future good things', Isaac says. 'A monk (ihidaya) is he who, making his dwelling far from the world's spectacles, has as the only entreaty of his prayer the desire for the world to come. A monk's wealth is the comfort that comes of mourning …' In accordance with this concept of the monk as mourner for sins, Isaac writes:

What meditation can a monk have in his cell save weeping? Could he have any time free from weeping to turn his gaze to another thought? And what occupation is better than this? A monk's very cell and his solitude, which bear a likeness to life in a tomb, far from human joys, teach him that his work is to mourn. And the very calling of his name urges and spurs him on to this, because he is called 'the mournful one' (abila), that is, bitter in heart. All the saints have left this life in mourning. If, therefore, all the saints mourned and their eyes were ever filled with tears till they departed from this life, who would have no need of weeping? A monk's consolation is born of his weeping. And if the perfect and victorious wept here, how could a man covered with wounds endure to abstain from weeping? He whose loved one lies dead before him and who sees himself dead in sins—has he need of instruction on the thought he should employ for tears? Your soul, slain by sins, lies before you; your soul which is of greater value to you than the whole world. Could there be no need for you to weep over her? If, therefore, we enter stillness and patiently persevere therein, we shall certainly by able to be constant in weeping. So let us entreat the Lord with an unrelenting mind to grant us mourning.

Thus mourning, Isaac teaches, should be constant and unceasing. As one comes closer to the fruit of spiritual life, tears become more and more frequent until they flow forth every day and every hour:

Question: What are the exact tokens and accurate signs that the fruit which is hidden in the soul has begun to appear from a man's labour?

Answer: When a man is deemed worthy to receive the gift of abundant tears which overcome him effortlessly. For tears are established for the mind as a kind of boundary between what is physical and what is spiritual and between passionateness and purity. Until a man receives this gift, the activity of his work is still in the outer man and he has not yet perceived at all the activity of the hidden things of the spiritual man. But when a man begins to relinquish the corporeal things of the present age and crosses this boundary to that which lies inside the visible nature, then straightway he will attain to the grace of tears. And from the first hospice of the hidden discipline tears begin to flow and they lead a man to perfection in the love of God. The more he progresses in this discipline, the more he is enriched with love, until by reason of his constant converse with tears he imbibes them with his food and drink.

At the same time constant weeping does not mark the climax of the spiritual journey. The culmination, according to Isaac, is the state wherein a person, under the influence of constant weeping, comes to 'peace of thought' and spiritual rest: in this state tears become 'moderate'. The dynamics of the transition from recurrent tears to constant weeping, and then from constant weeping to the 'moderate' tears of the perfect, is described by Isaac in Homily XIV of Part I: the advent of tears of repentance signifies that a person is embarking on the way to God. In the first stage of this way, tears are temporary and recurrent; in the second they flow without ceasing; in the highest, they come to a 'measure'. Isaac considers his teaching consonant with the faith of the whole Church:

When you attain to the region of tears, then know that your mind has left the prison of this world and has set its foot on the roadway of the new age, and has begun to breathe that other air, new and wonderful. And at the same moment it begins to shed tears, since the birth pangs of the spiritual infant are at hand. For grace, the common mother of all, makes haste mystically to give birth in the soul to the divine image for the light of the age to come.

Developing the same metaphor, Isaac teaches that before the infant has been born, tears come to a solitary from time to time, but once the infant is born, the tears increase as he grows up until they flow unceasingly: 'the eyes of such a man become like fountains of water for two years' time or even more, that is, during the time of transition'. After this transition, the person enters into the 'peace of thought' and the 'rest' of which Saint Paul spoke.

When you enter into that region which is peace of the thoughts, then the multitude of tears is taken away from you, and afterwards tears come to you in due measure and at the appropriate time. This is, in all exactness, the truth of the matter as told in brief, and it is believed by the whole Church and by her eminent men and front-line warriors.

Tears of repentance born from the consciousness of sins are accompanied by a 'bitterness of the heart' and contrition. But the dynamics of human development involves a gradual transition from this type of tears to another, to the sweet tears of compunction. Isaac expounds his teaching on the two types of tears in Homily XXXVII of Part I:

There are tears that burn and there are tears that anoint as if with oil, Isaac writes. All tears that flow out of contrition and an anguish of heart on account of sins dry up and burn the body, and often even the governing faculty feels the injury caused by their outflow. At first a man must necessarily come to this order of tears and through them a door is opened unto him to enter into the second order, which is superior to the first; this is the sign that a man has received mercy. These are the tears that are shed because of insight; they make the body comely and anoint it as if with oil, and they pour forth by themselves without compulsion. Not only do they anoint the body with oil, but they also alter a man's countenance. 'When the heart rejoiceth', he says, 'the countenance gloweth, but when it is in sorrows the countenance is downcast'. While the thinking is silent, these tears are poured forth over the entire countenance. The body receives from them a sort of nourishment, and gladness is imprinted upon the face. Someone who has had experience of these two alterations will understand.

The tears of compunction which are accompanied by the feeling of spiritual joy are granted to someone who attains purity of heart and dispassion. These tears, a consequence of the person's receiving revelations from above and the vision of God, are implied in the Beatitudes:

Blessed, therefore, are the pure in heart, for there is no time when they do not enjoy the sweetness of tears, and in this sweetness they see the Lord at all times. While tears are still wet in their eyes, they are deemed worthy of beholding his revelations at the height of their prayer; and they make no prayer without tears. This is the meaning of the Lord's saying, 'Blessed are they that mourn, for they shall be comforted'. For a man comes from mourning into purity of soul. But when the Lord said that they will be comforted, he did not explain what sort of comfort. When by means of tears a monk is deemed worthy of traversing the land of the passions and of reaching the plains of purity of soul, then he encounters there consolation which is not to be discovered in this world. Then he understands that this is the consolation received through purity at the completion of mourning, when God wills to give it to those who weep. For it is not possible that a man who continually mourns and weeps should be disquieted by the passions, since the gift of weeping and mourning belongs to the dispassionate. And if the tears of a man who weeps and mourns for a long time can not only lead him to dispassion, but even completely cleanse and free his mind of the memory of the passions, what can we say of those who night and day devote themselves to this activity? No one, therefore, accurately knows the help that comes of weeping, save only those who have surrendered their souls to this work. All the saints strive to reach this entryway, because by means of tears the door is opened for them to enter the land of consolation, where the footsteps of the love of God are imprinted through revelations.

Thus the tears of compunction which are born as someone reaches the state of purity and dispassion lead him to the perfection of the love of God. And the sign that a person has attained the love of God is his ability to shed tears every time when he remembers God:

Question: And whence does a man know that he has attained to the perfect love of God?

Answer: When the recollection of God is stirred in his mind, straightway his heart is kindled by the love of Him and his eyes pour forth abundant tears. For love is wont to ignite tears by the recollection of beloved ones. A man who is in this state will never be found destitute of tears, because that which brings him to the recollection of God is never absent from him; wherefore even in sleep he converses with God. For love is wont to cause such things.

Isaac often says that tears of compunction should accompany prayer. Tears during prayer are a sign that a person's repentance has been accepted by God. When the gift of tears is granted, Isaac warns, the delight of these tears should not be counted as idleness. A multitude of tears is born to a person in the life of stillness, 'sometimes with pain, sometimes with amazement; for the heart humbles herself and becomes like a tiny babe, and as soon as she begins to pray, tears flow in advance of her prayer'. By Isaac's testimony, tears during prayer were experienced by the majority of good monks of his time. A monk

may receive the gift of tears during the office—something which the majority of right-minded brethren experience—tears which by their quantity so compel that brother that he is unable to complete the office even though he struggles hard to do so: instead, he has to abandon the office because of abundant weeping …'

As we see, Isaac does not regard tears as an extraordinary gift, a special charisma of which only very few are counted worthy.

On the contrary, he is of the opinion that not only monks, but also persons in the world must shed tears of compunction.

What of those who are by nature incapable of or disinclined to tears? Isaac answers this question in Chapter XVIII of Part II. Continual weeping, he says, is born in a person for three reasons:

[First], as a result of wonder at the insights filled with mysteries that are revealed all the time to the intellect it can happen that abundant tears flow involuntarily without that person feeling any sorrow. ... Or tears may come from a fervent love of God which inflames the soul when someone can no longer endure without weeping continually as a result of its sweetness and delight. Or tears may come from an abundant lowliness of heart.

But if a person does not possess the flow of tears,

it is not just that he has no tears; rather, he is bereft of the things which cause tears and he does not possess in his soul those roots which give birth to them. In other words, he has never been aware of the taste of the love of God; reflection on the divine mysteries resulting from his continuance in God's presence has never stirred within him; nor does he possess lowliness of heart, even though he may imagine that he possesses humility.

When tears are absent, therefore, a person should not look for an excuse in the peculiarities of his nature. As true humility is not a natural quality but is acquired through the awareness of one's own unworthiness and remembrance of the Lord's humility, so in the same manner tears do not depend on nature but are a consequence of one of the three reasons mentioned above:

... If you do not possess lowliness of heart, or the sweet and burning suffering that comes with the love of God, things which are the root for those tears which pour forth delectable consolation in the heart, then do not take refuge in the excuse of any lameness on nature's part, or people whose heart is naturally torpid.

Where there is lowliness of heart and awareness of one's own unworthiness, there

it is not possible for that person to hold himself back from weeping, even though he does no want to. This is because the heart involuntary surges forth with a fountain of weeping continually, due to the burning feeling of suffering that is uncontrollably in it, and the contrition of heart.

Isaac does not always distinguish between the bitter tears of repentance and the sweet tears of compunction. The two types of tears are as two sides of a single coin, two aspects of one and the same experience. The tears of compunction, born from mystical insights, from the love of God, and from deep humility, are joyful tears. Yet at the same time they are accompanied by repentance, by the awareness of one's own sinfulness, by 'burning suffering' and a contrite heart.

———————————

CHAPTER VI

THE SCHOOL OF PRAYER

Just as nothing resembles God, so there is no ministry or work which resembles converse with God in stillness.

II/30,1

PRAYER IS UNDOUBTEDLY the most frequently discussed and most thoroughly developed theme in Saint Isaac. When reading his works, one receives a clear idea of how he and other members of the Church of the East prayed in his time: one can also gain a detailed picture of the theory and practice of prayer in the whole of the Eastern Christian tradition. This clarity is the reason why the writings of Isaac were a school of prayer for his contemporaries and remained—and still remain—such a school for many Christians in various parts of the world where Isaac's works are read and his recommendations put into practice.

In this chapter, after discussing Isaac's theory of prayer, we shall speak of various external aspects of prayer and then deal with the practice of prayer before the cross. The reading of Scripture and the night vigil will be analyzed as important constituents of the daily practice of prayer. We shall also point to Isaac's teaching on the rule of prayer, the universal character of prayer, and prayers for one's neighbour, the Church, and the world. In the concluding section, we will turn to the highest stages of prayer, when human prayer reaches the point of cessation and is transformed into contemplation.

1. PRAYER

'Prayer', according to Evagrius Ponticus, 'is the converse of the mind with God'. For Isaac the Syrian, the converse ('enyana) of the mind with God is the highest and most important spiritual activity of a Christian, and cannot be compared with any other endeavour: 'Just as nothing resembles God, so there is no ministry or work which resembles converse with God ('enyana d- 'am alaha) in stillness'. By prayer Isaac understands the whole range of activities which accompany the converse of the mind with God:

Every good care of the intellect directed toward God and every meditation upon spiritual things is delimited by prayer, is called by the name of prayer and under its name is comprehended; whether you speak of various readings, or the cries of a mouth glorifying God, or sorrowing reflection on the Lord, or making bows with the body, or the alleluias of psalmody, or all the other things from which the teaching of genuine prayer ensues.

According to the understanding traditional in Eastern Christian asceticism, prayer is the basis of a Christian's spiritual life, a source and cause of all good things. Isaac defines prayer as:

… the refuge of help, a source of salvation, a treasury of assurance, a haven that rescues from the tempest, a light to those who are in darkness, a staff of the infirm, a shelter in time of temptations, a medicine at the height of sickness, a shield of deliverance in war, an arrow sharpened against the face of the enemies, to speak simply: the entire multitude of these good things is found to have its entrance through prayer.

In another place, he defines prayer as 'the mind's freedom and rest from everything of this world and a heart that has completely turned its gaze toward the fervent desire belonging to the hope of future things'.

At the time of prayer, when a person's mind is collected and all the senses are brought into harmony, an encounter between God and the person praying takes place. This explains why all spiritual gifts and all mystical visions have been given to the saints at the time of prayer. It was during prayer that an angel appeared to Zacharias and announced the conception of John the Baptist; it was during the prayer of the sixth hour that Peter beheld the divine vision; it was while Cornelius the Centurion prayed that an angel appeared to him.

When the High Priest once a year, during the dread time of prayer, entered the Holy of Holies and cast himself down upon his face,… he heard the oracles of God through an awesome and ineffable revelation. O how awesome was the mystery which was ministered in this ceremony! So also at the time of prayer were all visions and revelations made manifest to the saints. For what other time is so holy, and by its sanctity so apt for the reception of gifts, as the time of prayer, wherein a man converses with God? At this time, when we make our petitions and our supplications to God, and we speak with him, a human being forcefully gathers together all the movements and deliberations of his soul and converses with God alone, and his heart is abundantly filled with God.

What are the main requirements which Isaac lays down for true prayer?

First, one should pray with attention and without distraction: external activity should not draw one's attention from prayer. Isaac cites as an example an ascetic who said: 'I was amazed when I heard of monks who do handwork in their cells and are able to perform their rule of prayer without omissions and remain free of turbulence. … I tell you in very truth, that if I go out to pass water, I am shaken from my habit of mind and its order and I am impeded from the accomplishment of my deeds of excellence'.

Secondly, one should pray with humility. The prayer of a humble person goes directly from his mouth to God's ear.

When you fall down before God in prayer, become in your thought like an ant, like a creeping thing of the earth, like a leech, and like a tiny lisping child. Do not say anything before him with knowledge, but with a child's manner of thought, draw near God and walk before him, that you may be counted worthy of that paternal providence that fathers have for their small children.

Thirdly, one should pray with deep affection and tears. The sense of the heart's affliction, accompanied by bodily labour—that is prostrations—should become an integral part of prayer: 'Reckon every prayer wherein the body does not toil and the heart is not afflicted to be a miscarriage, for this prayer has no soul'. At the same time, as Isaac quotes Evagrius, 'prayer is joy that sends up thanksgiving'. The paradoxical combination of affliction of the heart and the spiritual joy of thanksgiving becomes a source of tears, which accompany prayer, especially at its highest stages. 'The fullness of prayer is the gift of tears', Isaac says.

Tears during prayer is a sign that the soul has been deemed worthy of God's mercy in her repentance, and that her repentance has been accepted, and through her tears the soul has begun to enter into the plain of limpid purity

Fourthly, one should pray with a patience and an ardour that are connected with the love of God:

Love is a fruit of prayer that, by prayer's contemplation, draws the intellect insatiably toward that for which it longs when the intellect patiently perseveres in prayer without wearying, whether it prays in a visible way, employing the body, or with the mind's silent reflections, diligently and with ardour. Prayer is the mortification of the will's motions pertaining to the life of the flesh. For a man who prays correctly is the equal of the man who is dead to the world. And the meaning of 'to deny oneself is this: courageously to persevere in prayer.

Fifthly, every word of prayer should come from the depths of the heart. Even if the words of prayer are borrowed from the psalms, they should be uttered as if they were one's own:

In the verses of your psalmody do not be like a man who borrows words from another, lest … you be left utterly devoid of the compunction and joy to be found in psalmody. Rather, recite the words of psalmody as your very own, that you may utter the words of your supplication with insight and with discriminating compunction.

Isaac valued psalmody highly and emphasized the necessity of meditating on the words of psalms:

… The wondrous words set out in the Odes which are appointed in the Holy Church, along with all sorts of other lofty words set out by the Spirit in harmonious chants, all these can fulfill the place of perfect prayer in someone: by being meditated upon, they give birth within us to pure prayers and exalted insights, thus bringing us close to luminosity of mind and wonder at God, as well as to all the other things with which the Lord will enlighten you with wisdom in their due time, as you select those verses that are appropriate and offer them up to your Lord with supplication as your intention, repeating them at length and serenely.

Finally, prayer should be based on faith and absolute trust in God. Thus we may not ask God for earthly goods, which God will give us even without our making a special request:

Do not ask of God a thing which he himself, without our asking, has already taken forethought to give … to us. … A son does not ask bread of his father, but seeks the great and lofty things of his father's house. It was on account of the feebleness of the minds of common men that the Lord commanded us to ask for our daily bread, for mark what he commanded to those who are perfect in knowledge and healthy in soul: 'Take no thought concerning food and raiment… . But seek ye rather the kingdom of God and its righteousness, and all these things will be added unto you'.

Those who truly believe in God do not ask God 'Give this to us', or 'Take that from us', and do not take heed of themselves at all, for they perceive in their life the fatherly providence of God. Instead of asking God 'What will you give me?', the freeborn soul asks God to preserve the treasury of faith in its heart, 'though in fact God does not need even this prayer'.

The main requirements necessary for prayer, according to Isaac, are therefore: attentiveness and the absence of distraction, humility, a deep feeling of contrition accompanied by tears, patience, and ardor, words of prayer uttered out of the depths of the heart, true belief, and trust in God. Such prayer will easily and speedily reach the ears of God.

Sometimes, however, God may appear to be slow in answering prayer and not always to fulfill requests. Isaac gives two reasons for this. The first is the providence of God, by which God gives to everyone according to his measure and ability to receive:

If you should beseech God for a thing and he is slow to hearken to you speedily, do not grieve, for you are not wiser than God. This happens to you either because you are not worthy to obtain your request, or because the pathways of your heart do not accord with your petitions, but rather the contrary, or because your hidden measure is too immature for the greatness of the thing you are asking for.

Another reason why God seems not to hear our prayer is our own sins:

Since we say that God is plenteous in mercy, why is it that when amidst temptations we unceasingly knock and pray, we are not heard and he disregards our prayer? This we are clearly taught by the Prophet when he says: 'The Lord's hand is not little, that it cannot save; nor is he heavy of hearing, that he cannot hear: but our sins have separated us from him, and our iniquities have turned away his face that he doth not hearken'. Remember God at all times, and he will remember you whenever you fall into evils.

2. OUTWARD ASPECTS OF PRAYER

Widespread opinion holds that an interest in the external aspects of ascetical activity and the practice of prayer is not characteristic of the mystical writers; they allegedly concentrate only on the inner fruits of this practice. Isaac the Syrian is one of many writers who prove how misleading this idea is. We find in his works many descriptions of outward forms of prayer based on his own practice and that of the solitaries of his time. To cite just one example:

One person may spend the entire day in prayer and in reading Scripture, giving over only a small part to standing in the recitation of the Psalter, in this way best increasing in himself the continual recollection of God. Another person may be occupied the whole day solely in psalmody, without specifically being aware at all of prayer. Yet another may occupy himself night and day just with frequent kneelings, incorporating the distinctive limits of the Hours and Office prayers within his frequent kneelings, without marking them off. ... And occasionally, standing up from there for a while at peace in his heart, he will turn himself for a little to meditating on Scripture. Yet another person may occupy the entire day in reading Scripture, his aim being to forget this transient world and to be dead in his mind to the recollection of its transient affairs. ... Delighting in the insights of divine mysteries and in wonder at God's dispensation at every moment, he will give himself over for a little to standing in prayer and psalmody. But the portion of his reading is greater than that of prayer.

In this passage, several outward forms of prayer are listed, such as psalmody, reading, kneeling. Isaac attaches great value to kneelings (prostrations), considering them as one of the most important spiritual exercises: 'More than the practice of psalmody, love prostrations during prayer'. Isaac recommends that an ascetic make many prostrations during prayer:

At whatever time God should open up your thinking from within, give yourself over to unremitting bows and prostrations. ... There is nothing greater and more laborious in ascetical struggles, and nothing more excites envy in the demons, than if a man prostrates himself before the cross of Christ, praying night and day, and is like a convict whose hands are bound behind him.

As an example of how prayer should be accompanied by many prostrations, Isaac cites the night prayer of one monk whom he visited: '... It was impossible for me to count the number of his prostrations. Indeed, who could number the prostrations which that brother made every night?'

Another external action which can accompany prayer is striking the head with the hand. This, or a similar, practice seems to be widespread not only in the syrian tradition, but in oriental monasticism in general. 'Tears, striking the head in prayer with the hand, and casting oneself with fervour upon the earth', Isaac says, 'waken the warmth of ... sweetness inside the heart, and with a laudable ecstasy the heart soars up toward God ...' Isaac also speaks of striking one's head upon the ground 'a hundred times or more'. He emphasizes that every ascetic employs one or another form of ascetical practice during prayer, for there is no common rule for everyone. But his regard for beating one's head as a possible substitute for the whole sequence of daily monastic offices is quite intriguing:

The diverse works of those who live according to God are the following: one man strikes his head all the day long, and does this instead of the hours of his services. Another joins together the set number of his prayers by persevering in continual prostrations. Another replaces services by copious tears and this suffices him. ... But another, having tested but a little of these things, became puffed up and fell into error.

Those who 'became puffed up' refers to the Messalians. Isaac was generally not interested in polemics: he avoided, for example, the discussion of any christological points which might have caused controversy among his readers. We do, however, find in his writings polemical statements against messalian opinions. The messalian movement—a name taken from the syriac mhallyane, 'those who pray'—appeared in the fourth century and spread over the entire Christian Orient. Messalians rejected the Church's sacraments and asceticism: prayer was considered as the main spiritual activity, and by means of it, the Messalians claimed, one reaches various ecstatic states. As a mystical writer who developed themes connected with the practice of prayer and spiritual life, Isaac was sensitive to the manifestations of false mysticism and to all sorts of corruption of the practice of prayer, and keenly reacted to the 'messalian errors'.

Among Isaac's writings dedicated to anti-messalian polemics, Chapter XIV of Part II occupies first place. Called 'On prayer and its outward forms', it contains many precious indications of how the syrian monks of Isaac's time prayed.

Though the state of perfection consists in having obtained spiritual gifts and attained pure prayer, nobody should neglect outward forms of prayer, states Isaac. Reverential outward postures are conducive to one's inward progress towards pure prayer:

If someone decides to abandon what belongs in first place, without having found what comes afterwards, then it is clear that he is being mocked by the demons. ... It is in proportion to the honour which someone shows in his person to God during the time of prayer, both with his body and the mind, that the door to assistance will be opened for him, leading to the purifying of the impulses and to illumination in prayer. Someone who shows a reverential posture during prayer, by stretching out his hands to heaven as he stands in modesty, or by falling on his face to the ground, will be accounted worthy of great grace from on high. Anyone who continuously adorns his prayer with such outward postures will swiftly and quickly be accounted worthy of the activity of the Holy Spirit, for the Lord is accounted great in his eyes, thanks to the honour he shows in the sacrifices which he presents before the Lord at those times which have been set apart for him by the law of freewill.

Isaac emphasizes at the same time that God does not need our external signs of reverence. A reverential outward posture is necessary for us, however, so that we may be trained in a reverent attitude to God:

You should realize, my brothers, that in all our service God very much wants outward postures, specific kinds of honour, and visible forms of prayer—not for his own sake, but for our benefit. He himself is not profited by such things, nor does he lose anything when they are neglected; rather, they are for the sake of our feeble nature. Had such things not been requisite, he himself would not have adopted such outward postures during his incarnation—thus speaking with us in the Holy Scriptures. He cannot be dishonoured by anything, seeing that honour belongs to him by his very nature. But we, as a result of slovenly habits and various outward actions which lack reverence, have acquired an attitude of mind that shows contempt towards him. Consequently we fall from grace of our own volition, seeing that we are subject to backsliding: then we are assailed by incessant attacks and continual deception from the demons, as we acquire a nature that loves comfort and is easily swayed to evil actions.

Having substantiated the need for outward forms of prayer, Isaac turns to a direct attack on messalian practice:

Many people have despised these outward postures in their thoughts and supposed that prayer of the heart suffices by itself for God, claiming, as they lie on their backs or are sitting in a disrespectful manner, that there should only be an interior recollection of God; they are not concerned at all with adorning the visible side of their worship with prolonged standing, corresponding to their body's strength, or with making the venerable sign of the cross over their organs of the senses. Nor are they concerned, as they kneel on the ground, to act like those about to draw near to a flame and themselves assume, both inwardly and outwardly, a reverential posture, or to accord especial honour to the Lord, honouring him with all their limbs and with reverence on their faces. This is because they have not perceived the might of the adversary they have, and as a result they are handed over to the workings of falsehood, not having understood that they are still mortal and liable to be stirred by their soul, which is subject to backsliding; they do not realize that they have not yet reached the state of spiritual beings, or that the resurrection has not yet taken place and they have not yet achieved a state of immutability. During the body's life, when human nature is in need of labour and training in new things all the time, they have wanted to lead their lives in a purely spiritual state, without being involved in those things which necessarily daily constrain the world which is subject to the passions. 'Imagining in themselves that they are wise, they have acted with disrespect', in that the sign of pride and disrespect for

God has appeared in them. As a result they have doubled their perdition by means of prayer—which is properly the fountainhead of all life. This is because they supposed they could offer disrespect to the Honourable One who is not to be disrespected and who is to be honoured by all created beings.

By their neglect of outward forms of prayer, claims Isaac, the Messalians placed themselves in opposition to Church tradition. The ancient Fathers not only prayed in their heart, but also observed various external rules and cared about the posture of the body during prayer:

It was not the case, as detractors say, that these fixed numbers of prayers related concerning them were prayers which just took place in the heart; this is what people with messalian opinions proclaim concerning them, those who say that outward forms of worship are unnecessary.

The Holy Fathers, Isaac continues, prayed with reverence, falling down before the cross, making prostrations, kissing the cross, and sometimes spending hours on their knees:

These Fathers' acts of worship were very real, and in particular, by means of them their soul was kept humble. They carried them all out, taking care to stand up from their places as they did so—provided they were not prevented by physical weakness—with great reverence and deep lowliness of both mind and body, lying prostrate on their faces before the cross. These acts of worship were quite separate from those which took place in the heart. Nevertheless, each time they stood up, they performed many acts of worship, their body assisting them as the occasion might allow, kissing the cross five or maybe ten times, reckoning each act of worship and kiss as a single prayer. During such acts someone might all of a sudden sometimes discover a pearl which in a single prayer would encompass the number of all the others. Sometimes a person would be standing on his feet, or kneeling, his mind seized by the wonder of prayer—a state not under the control of the will of flesh and blood and the soul's impulses. Or he might be in one of those states of purity of prayer which we will elucidate later.

Isaac then discusses in greater detail how the Fathers counted the prayers they performed daily. They said many prayers and made many prostrations, he suggests, but did not stand up for each prostration and did not sit down after each prayer. Having once stood up, they would make many prostrations, and then, after finishing, they would read Scripture, or recite the service, or pray with tears:

In this manner the Fathers used to carry out those large numbers of prayers, just as I have described. It was not, as many people suppose and as others also claim, that they distinguished a separate time of standing for each prayer individually—for the wretched body is not capable of such numbers, standing up separately for each separate prayer. On this reckoning all the prayers would never be achieved if someone wanted to stand up from his place a hundred times in a day, or fifty, or sixty times—to say nothing of three hundred times or more, as was the custom of some of the saints; otherwise there would have been no room for reading or any of the other requirements. Nor would there have been any opportunity for prolonging prayer, should it happen that during someone's prayer, the gift of tears were granted by grace or a limpid stirring to draw out one's prayer, as happens with those who have been counted worthy of one of these kinds of grace at such times. Instead, such a person's Office would be turbulent and he would be filled with turmoil in all his ministry.

Then Isaac suggests that his reader experience the effect of various ways of prayer in order to see how impossible it is to stand up separately for each and every prayer:

If someone does not believe this, let him experiment on himself and see whether he can get up tranquilly from his place fifty times during a day—let alone a hundred or two hundred times—and remain undisturbed in himself and his prayer peaceful, as well as fulfil his Office and the appointed scriptural reading—which constitutes a large part of prayer—still unperturbed; will he manage to do this for a whole week—let alone all the days of his life?

Isaac records all these statements on the practice of prayer because, in opposition to Messalianism, he wants to leave his disciples a detailed manual of prayer. The Messalians, he continues, reject not only external forms of prayer, but also the sacraments of the Church and the reading of Scripture. This break with the tradition of the Church led the Messalians to spiritual error, pride, and demonic beguilement:

It is not continual prayer which is the cause of going astray, nor the omission of some psalms—provided there is an appropriate reason for this; nor do we go on to account prayer—the source of life—and the labour involved in it as something which leads to error. Rather, error came when certain people abandoned prayer's venerable outward forms, turning instead to their own rules and special customs which they had laid down for themselves according to their own whim, and when they completely deprived themselves of the Holy Mysteries, instead despising and scorning them; when they deprived themselves furthermore of the light of the divine Scriptures and failed to study the teaching of the words of the Fathers which give instructions about the stratagems against the demons; and when they gave up the various acts of lowliness, prostrations, continual falling upon the ground, a suffering heart and the submissive postures appropriate to prayer, modest standing, hands clasped in submissive fashion, or stretched out to heaven, the senses respectful during prayer. Instead, they seized upon various forms of pride, as a result mingling with their prayer insult towards God. They accompanied their prayer with haughty outward postures, forgetting how exalted is the Divine Nature and how their own nature is but dust. Yet in all this the words of their prayer were no different from those of the psalms.

Continuing his description of the outward forms of prayer, Isaac then comes to prayer with outstretched hands. This posture, according to him, promotes concentration of thought and a deep feeling of compunction. Isaac also emphasizes the necessity of prayer with one's own words; this prayer, he is convinced, leads to spiritual insights:

Most prayers, in fact, consist of words chosen from psalms containing ideas and sentiments of grief and supplication, or of thanksgiving and praise, on so on. Thus sometimes, when someone is kneeling with his face bowed or has his fingers and gaze raised to heaven, he will add his own feeling to the words and repeat them slowly. On occasion the suffering and pain of his heart will cause all sorts of deeply-felt words of prayer to spring up, or joy may burst forth in response to something, stirring that person to alter his prayer to praises owing to the delight his mind feels. The same applies to other stirrings at prayer which the Holy Spirit sets in motion in the saints, in whose utterances are ineffable mysteries and insights. And when the outward form of prayer provides some sign of the insight they contain, this is an indication of the mysteries and perfect knowledge which the saints receive mingled into their prayers through the wisdom of the Spirit.

The advantage of praying in one's own words is that it does not require the recitation of texts from a book or learning texts by heart and repeating them. Some ancient saints, Isaac notes, did not know the psalms at all, yet their prayer, unlike that of the Messalians, reached God because of their humility:

A person either draws near God or he falls away from truth; this depends on the direction in which his mind is aimed and not on the external features of what is done or neglected. Many of the early Fathers—I refer to some of the great solitaries—did not even know the psalms, yet their prayers ascended to God like fire as a result of their excellent ways and the lowliness of mind which they had acquired. Their words chased away demons like flies; they buzzed off as they approached. Many people, however, have used prayer as an excuse for slackness and pride: failing to grasp the better part, they also lost the part they had. Though they held nothing in their hands, they imagined that they stood in a state of perfection. Others, merely on the basis of the educational training they have had, have supposed that this would be enough to enable them to discover knowledge of truth: relying on secular culture and ordinary reading, they fell away from truth, and failed to humble themselves so as to stand up again.

We see what meaning outward forms of prayer held for Isaac. He was convinced that prayer with all its outward forms is 'the fulfillment of all virtues'.

At the same time he understands that outward forms, however important they may be, are only an aid in acquiring pure prayer. Outside the context of the anti-messalian polemic he speaks of the necessity of outward forms in a much more reserved manner. In particular, he accepts prayer while sitting. Especially for the old and the sick, there must be special rules which exclude bodily labour:

We do not force the sick or the infirm to abide by the rule, nor do we say that we should subject someone to impossibilities. Everything that takes place with reverence and trembling, and as a result of the exigency of the occasion, is seen by God as a choice offering, even if it lies outside the norm of the rule. Not only does he attach no blame to the person who so acts, but he accepts paltry and insignificant things done with a good will for his sake along with mighty and perfect actions.

Outward forms of prayer are necessary, but they should be measured in accordance with the strength of each person. It is not only the old and infirm who are freed from the necessity of performing many prostrations and other external actions of prayer. Anyone who is grown tired in prayer deserves a rest:

Once you have grown feeble and become weary as a result of the labour of psalmody … and as a result of old age or of great infirmity of body, you are no longer able to toil at this as you once did, then toil instead in supplication and intercession, and things like these. Offer up your supplication at length and earnestly; make your requests with care, and toil on your supplication with the toil of the heart. Be importunate, extend your prayer and hold out until the door is opened to you. For our Lord is merciful and he will receive you—not on the basis of your labour, but in accordance with the direction of your mind. Then your soul will become illumined as you extend your supplication and your thoughts will be enflamed with love of him. In this way you will receive assistance from God in the meagre labours that your weak body undertakes, without, so far as possible, completely abandoning your curtailed Offices—so that you do not appear to be like someone who is unwilling to be subjected to the monastic rule, for that would result in the demon of pride assaulting you, as happens with the person who imagines that he no longer needs such things; or you will gradually end up in a state of voluntary lassitude. I am not imposing any necessary time limit: rather, I am speaking of what can happen and take place.

One can pray standing, sitting, or kneeling; what is important is that prayer should be offered in the fear of God:

Nor would it be anything blameworthy if, in accordance with the time that corresponds with our strength—and it does not even need to correspond—we are standing or sitting, provided that great awe and wakefulness accompany us, thus preventing any contempt of God from entering us at the time when his Office is being performed by us, or when the sacrifice of prayer is being made before him. Rather, this is a matter of understanding and discernment, and not of fixed limits and confusion, without your being too greatly concerned with quantity—for this often enough proves to be the cause of inner turbulence. Instead, our aim should be to find a way by which our heart can draw near to God in the Office and in prayer: this is the purpose of your being subject to the law that appertains to children. But even more than psalmody, add these other things and make special use of them, sometimes standing on your feet, sometimes kneeling, sometimes, again, seated.

Ultimately, Isaac comes to the conclusion that there are no outward postures that are inevitably requisite during prayer. A deliberate rejection of outward forms of prayer may cause someone to fall into pride and the 'messalian error'. Yet this does not imply that it is completely impossible to pray without outward forms. On the contrary, one should pray at any time and in any physical posture:

A person can be occupied at this while standing up or sitting down, while working or while walking inside his cell, while he is going to sleep, until the point when sleep takes over, while he is indoors or while he is traveling on a journey, secretly occupying himself with them within his heart; likewise, while he is constantly kneeling on the ground, or wherever he happens to be standing, even if it is not in front of the cross... .

3. PRAYER BEFORE THE CROSS

In several of the passages quoted above, Isaac mentions prayer and prostrations before the cross, kissing the cross, and other signs of special reverence which a Christian must show to the cross. Isaac's frequent references to the cross reflect the exceptional place that the holy cross occupies in syriac Christianity. The Church of the East at the time of Isaac did not have a developed tradition of icon-painting. Though various types of icons had existed in this Church since a very early date, the cult of the cross was much more developed. The Church of the East surrounded the holy cross with devotional and liturgical veneration as a symbol of human salvation and of God's invisible presence. In this respect Isaac's teaching on prayer before the cross is of special interest, for it allows us to come into contact with the ancient tradition of the Syrian Orient and to see what the importance of the cross was in the spiritual life of Isaac's compatriots and contemporaries.

Saint Isaac's teaching on the holy cross as a symbol of divine dispensation and an object of religious veneration is expounded in Chapter XI of Part II, under the heading 'On the contemplation of the mystery of the cross; and on what power it conveys in an invisible way in its visible form, and on the vast mysteries of God's governance which were performed in the ancients, and the summing up of this in Christ our Lord; and how the all-powerful cross conveys the sum of this'. The text begins with a question which contains clear indications of the universal character of the veneration of the cross in the syrian tradition: 'In what sense, and whose type is it that the image of the cross depicts for us—this image which is held in great honour by us and which is gladly venerated by us with love and insatiable desire; whose story is known to and repeated by, as it were, the whole world?' In an introductory paragraph Isaac makes clear his intention to speak of the action of the power of God in different epochs of human history; and of how God 'places his honoured name in an awesome way upon corporeal objects in every generation, manifesting in them wondrous and magnificent things to the world, granting by their means great benefits to humanity'; and finally of the eternal power which is in the cross.

As he begins his exposition, Isaac emphasizes that there is no special power in the cross different from that power through which the worlds were brought into being and which governs all of creation in accordance with God's will. In the cross lives the very same power that lived in the ark of the covenant, regarded with awesome veneration by the people of Israel:

The limitless power of God dwells in the cross, just as it resided in an incomprehensible way in the ark which was venerated amidst great honour and awe by the jewish people, performing by it miracles and awesome signs in the midst of those who were not ashamed to call it 'God', that is, they would gaze upon it in awe as though upon God, because of the glory of God's honoured name which was upon it. This ark was honoured with this name not only by the jewish people, but by foreign peoples, their enemies: 'Woe to us, for the God of the People has come to the camp today'. That power which existed in the ark is believed by us to exist in this revered form of the cross, which we hold in honour in great awareness of God.

What was in the ark, Isaac asks, that made it so awesome and filled with powers and signs? The ark was venerated, he answers, because the invisible Shekhina (Presence) of God dwelt in it: 'Did not Moses and the People prostrate before the ark in great awe and trembling? Did not Joshua son of Nun lie stretched out on his face before it from morning until evening? Were not God's fearsome revelations manifested there, as if to afford honour to this object, seeing that the Shekhina of God was residing in it?' The very same Shekhina now resides in the Holy Cross: it has departed from the Old Testament ark and entered the New Testament cross. This is why the miracles of the Apostles, which are described in the New Testament, were more powerful than those performed in Old Testament times:

Through the power of the cross many have restrained wild animals, acted boldly in the face of fire, walked on lakes, raised the dead, held back plagues, caused springs to flow in parched and wild terrain, set a boundary to the seas, commanded the surge of mighty rivers to flow after them, and reversed the course of water. Why do I speak of these things? Satan himself and all his tyranny is in terror of the form of the cross, when it is depicted by us against him.

The Old Testament cult with all its signs and wonders, Isaac continues, was unable to eradicate sin, whereas the cross destroyed the power of sin. The cross also destroyed the power of death:

And as for death, which had been so fearful for human nature, now even women and children can hold up their heads against it. Death which reigns over all has now proved easier, not only for believers, but also for pagans as well: fear of it has been greatly diminished from what had been the case previously.

In other words, the religion of the cross brought into the world a different attitude to death: it is no longer feared, as it once was in pre-christian times. Does this passage contain a reference to the epoch of martyrdom, when women and children faced death? According to Isaac, christian tranquillity in the face of death influenced pagan society as well: the attitude to death became less dramatic.

Returning to Old Testament images, Isaac asks why it was that before the construction of the wooden ark, built by the hands of carpenters, 'adoration filled with awe was offered up continuously', in spite of the prohibition of the Law against worshipping the work of human hands or any image or likeness? Because in the ark, Isaac answers, unlike in the pagan idols, the power of God was manifested openly and the name of God was set upon it. Turning to the veneration of the cross, Isaac therefore sweeps aside the accusation of idolatry, the very same accusation that was brought up against iconodules in Byzantium in the eighth century. Though in the byzantine polemic against iconoclasm the main argument for the veneration of icons was the Incarnation of God the Word which made possible the depiction of God in material colours—a theme not touched upon by Isaac—in general Isaac's idea of the presence of the Godhead in material objects has much in common with what byzantine polemicists of his time were writing on the presence of God in icons. In particular, Isaac says, if the cross were made not 'in the name of that Man in whom the Divinity dwells'—that is, the Incarnate God the Word—the accusation of idolatry would have been justified. He also alludes to the interpretation of the 'Orthodox Fathers', according to whom the metal leaf which was placed above the ark of the convenant was a type of the human nature of Christ.

Isaac emphasizes that the divine Presence-Shekhina always accompanies the cross, from the very moment of its depiction:

The moment this form is depicted on a wall or on a board, or is fashioned out of some kind of gold or silver and the like, or carved out of wood, immediately it takes on and is filled with the divine power ... and so it becomes a place of God's Shekhina, even more so than the ark.

This passage contains important evidence concerning various types of the cross used in the syrian tradition. It also points to the practice of the ancient Church which knew no special prayers for the consecration of a cross: it was believed that, as soon as the cross is made or depicted, it becomes a source of sanctification for people and a place of divine presence. Consequently:

whenever we gaze upon this image in the time of prayer, or when we show reverence to it, because that Man was crucified upon it, we receive divine power through it and we are held worthy of assistance, salvation, and ineffable good in this world and in the world to come... .

Old Testament symbols were only a type and shadow of New Testament realities, according to Isaac, who emphasises the superiority of the cross over Old Testament representations:

Just as the ministry of the New Covenant is more honourable before God than the things which took place in the Old Covenant, just as there is a difference between Moses and Christ, just as the ministry which Jesus exercised is more excellent that the one given through Moses … so this form of the cross which now exists is far more honourable because of the honour of the Man whom the Godhead took from us as his abode; and because the divine good pleasure which is in this Man who completely became its temple is different from the metaphorical good pleasure which of old was in those inarticulate objects which foreshadowed these things to come in Christ.

The Old Testament cult required a devout and fearful attitude towards sacred objects. Whenever the priest entered the ark, 'he did not dare raise his eyes and examine it, for the awesome Shekhina of the Divinity was in it'. But if the type was so fearful and honourable, how much more honourable should be 'the very archetype to whom belong all symbols and types'. At the same time, the veneration offered to sacred objects in the Old Testament was caused by fear of the punishment to which everyone who showed disrespect to them was subject. In the New Testament, on the contrary, 'grace without measure has been poured out, and severity has been swallowed up by gentleness, and a familiarity of speech (parresia)… has been born. … And familiarity of speech is in the habit of chasing away fear, thanks to the abundant kindness of God which has come upon us at this time'.

We venerate the cross, therefore, not out of fear of punishment, but because of our fearful love of Christ, who accomplished our salvation through the cross. In contemplating the cross, Christians see Christ himself:

For true believers the sign of the cross is no small thing, for all symbols are understood to be contained within it. But whenever they raise their eyes and gaze on it, it is as though they were contemplating the face of Christ, and accordingly they are filled with reverence for it: the sight of it is precious and fearsome to them, and at the same time, beloved. … And whenever we approach the cross, it is as though we are brought close to the body of Christ: this is what it seems to us to be in our faith in him. And by drawing near to him, and gazing towards him, straightway we travel in our intellects to heaven, mystically. As though at some sight that cannot be seen or sensed, and out of honour for our Lord's humanity, our hidden vision is swallowed up through a certain contemplation of the mystery of faith.

We venerate the cross in the name of Christ and because of Christ. In general, all that belonged to Christ as a Man should be venerated by us as having been raised up to the level of God, who wanted the man Christ to share in the glory of his Godhead. All this became clear to us on the cross, and it is through the cross that we acquire an accurate knowledge of the Creator.

The material cross, whose type was the ark of the covenant, is, in turn, the type of the eschatological kingdom of Christ. The cross, as it were, links the Old Testament with the New, and the New with the age to come, when all material symbols and types will be abolished. The whole economy of Christ, which began in Old Testament times and will continue until the end of the world, is encompassed in the symbol of the cross:

For the cross is Christ's garment just as the humanity of Christ is the garment of the Divinity. Thus the cross today serves as a type, awaiting the time when the true prototype will be revealed: then those things will not be required any longer. For the Divinity dwells inseparably in the Humanity, without any end, and for ever; in other words, boundlessly For this reason we look on the cross as the place belonging to the Shekhina of the Most High, the Lord's sanctuary, the ocean of the symbols of God's economy. This form of the cross manifests to us, by means of the eye of faith, the symbol belonging to the two Testaments. ... Moreover, it is the final seal of the economy of our Saviour. Whenever we gaze on the cross, ... the recollection of our Lord's entire economy gathers together and stands before our interior eyes.

The Chapter ends with the hymn of thanksgiving to God who eternally had the intention of giving the true knowledge to humanity by means of the cross, a material symbol of his economy:

Blessed is God who uses corporeal objects continually to draw us close in a symbolic way to a knowledge of his invisible nature. ... Let our hearts rejoice in the mysteries of the faith which we hold; let us exult in God who is so concerned with us. ... How much to be worshipped is the God who, for our salvation, has done everything in the world to bring us close to him, before the time when what has been prepared will be revealed. ... How much to be worshipped is the symbol of the cross, seeing that it has given to us all these things, and through it we have been deemed worthy of the knowledge of angels—that is, through the power by which all created things, both visible and invisible, were created.

This is the 'theology of the cross' expounded by Isaac in Chapter XI of Part II. It can be summed up in the following propositions: **1)** the ark of the covenant was a type of the cross; **2)** the Shekhina-Presence of God resides in the cross, having passed there from the ark of the covenant; **3)** veneration of the cross is not idolatry, because Christ is present in the cross, and the veneration is directed to him and not to a material object; **4)** the cross is a symbol of God's economy concerning human beings; **5)** the cross is a type of the reality of the age to come, where all material symbols will be abolished.

In the syrian tradition in general and in Saint Isaac in particular, we see that the cross is in fact the main and the only sacred picture which becomes an object of liturgical veneration. If, in the byzantine tradition, various stages of Christ's economy, as well as different heroes of biblical and Church history (the prophets, apostles, saints) might have been depicted variously in icons, for a Syrian Christian all this variety of iconography was replaced by the image of the cross. Theirs is an extremely concentrated and ascetic vision, which does not need different painted images. In the syriac tradition prayer is, as it were, focused on one point, and this point was the cross of Christ.

When Isaac remarks that it is possible to pray while 'not even in front of the cross', he reveals that the prayer before the cross was regarded as an invariable part of the practice of prayer. Prayer in front of the cross was so commonly accepted that the prayer not in front of it required special apology.

Isaac also describes different forms of prayer before the cross. One of them (already mentioned above) consists in lying prostrate before the cross in silence for a long time. During periods of grace, Isaac writes, all rules of prayer can be replaced by lying face down before the cross:

Is it not clear from the fact that you are lying prostrate before the cross for most of the day—a form of prayer which encompasses within itself all partial prayer and the office—that this prayer has made the canons subordinate to you? ... In the case of someone who is clinging to God unceasingly in the continual outpouring that takes place in prayer, constantly stretched out on the ground in supplication to him, his soul swallowed up with yearning as he lies fallen before the cross—this person is not subject to any law or canonical rules, nor do times and specific appointed periods have any authority over him; rather, he is from that point on above them, being with God without any limitation.

Lying prostrate before the cross, according to Isaac, is a form of prayer higher than all others, for, being an experience of extreme concentration and collectedness which is accompanied by the intensive feeling of God's presence, it encompasses all others within itself.

Another form of prayer before the cross consisted of raising one's eyes and continually 'gazing' upon the cross: this prayer can be accomplished while standing or sitting, as well as while kneeling with hands stretched out. Isaac describes a man who 'bends his knees in prayer and stretches forth his hands to the heavens, fixing his eyes upon the cross of Christ and concentrating all his thoughts on God during prayer'. In other place he speaks of 'insight into the Crucified' during prayer before the cross. Does he mean here a crucifix, the cross with the image of the crucified Christ, or a simple cross without any image, which is a symbol of the invisible presence of the Crucified One? Probably the second: insight into Christ present in the cross in an invisible manner. The popularity of images of the crucified Christ in Byzantium did not spread to the syrian tradition. It was not by chance that Isaac suggested, in a passage quoted above, that whenever believers raise their eyes to gaze on the cross, it is as though they see Christ himself, that is, they do not see a representation of Christ with their physical eyes; they see Christ with the eyes of the intellect and heart.

Isaac also speaks of prostrations before the cross: both multiple prostrations and a single extended prostration. In one passage he mentions Christians enduring

… hunger, reading, all-night and sober vigil, according to a man's strength, and the numerous prostrations we are obliged to make both during the hours of the day and also frequently at night. Some make thirty prostrations at a time, and afterward kiss the precious cross and then withdraw from it. There are those who add to this number according to their own capacity. And there are others who stay three hours in one prayer and without effort possess a vigilant intellect and no wandering of thoughts while they cast themselves upon their faces.

Kissing the cross many times is yet another form of the veneration of the cross. After making prostrations, the ancient Fathers kissed the cross five or ten times. Isaac tells us of the prayer of a solitary at whose house he happened to spend the night when he was ill:

… I saw this brother's custom of rising at night before the other brethren to begin his prayer rule. He would recite the psalms until suddenly he would leave off his rule and, falling upon his face, he would strike his head upon the ground a hundred times or more with fervour kindled in his heart by grace. Then he would stand up, kiss the cross of the Master, again make a prostration, again kiss the same cross, and again throw himself upon his face. … He would kiss the cross some twenty times with fear and ardour, with love mingled with reverence, and then begin again to recite the psalms.

It is evident that the practice of venerating the cross and prayer before the cross was one of the most important constituents of Isaac's teaching on prayer.

4. READING

Another important practice was the prayerful recitation, or 'reading' (qeryana), which is often mentioned or described by Isaac. This term refers primarily, though not exclusively, to the reading of Scripture. For Isaac, as for the whole of ancient monastic tradition, the reading of Scripture is not so much study of the biblical text with a cognitive aim as converse, encounter, revelation: the text of the Bible is a means by which we can directly experience converse with God, a mystical encounter which bestows insights into the depths of the divine reality.

Isaac speaks of reading Scripture as the chief means of a spiritual transformation that is accompanied by a rejection of sinful life:

The beginning of the path of life is continually to exercise the intellect in the words of God, and to live in poverty. ... There is nothing so capable of banishing the inherent tendencies of licentiousness from our soul, and of driving away those active memories which rebel in our flesh and produce a turbulent flame, as to immerse oneself in the fervent love of instruction, and to search closely into the depth of the insights of divine Scriptures. When a man's thoughts are totally immersed in the delight of pursuing the wisdom treasured in the words of Scripture by means of the faculty that gains enlightenment from them, then he puts the world behind his back and forgets everything in it. ... Often he does not even remember the employment of the habitual thoughts which visit human nature, and his soul remains in ecstasy by reason of those new encounters that arise from the sea of the Scripture's mysteries.

Scripture and patristic literature are the two kinds of reading recommended by Isaac:

We should consider the labour of reading to be something extremely elevated; its importance cannot be exaggerated. For it serves as the gate by which the intellect enters into the divine mysteries and takes strength for attaining luminosity in prayer: it bathes with enjoyment as it wanders over the acts of God's dispensation which have taken place for the benefit of humanity. ... From these acts prayer is illumined and strengthened—whether it be that they are taken from the spiritual Scriptures, or from things written by the great teachers in the Church on the topic of the divine dispensation; or among those who teach the mysteries of the ascetic life. These two kinds of reading are useful for the man of the spirit. ... Without reading the intellect has no means of drawing near to God: Scripture draws the mind up and sets it at every moment in the direction of God; it baptizes it from this corporeal world with its insights and causes it to be above the body continually. There is no other toil by which someone can make better progress. Provided that person is reading Scripture for the sake of the truth, these are the sorts of things he will discover from it.

Reading Scripture and the Fathers—as well as the lives of the saints—is, like prayer, conversation with God. Isaac recommends alternating prayer and reading, so that, during prayer, ideas drawn from Scripture fill the mind. Passing in this way from one kind of converse to another, a person constantly holds within his mind the memory of God:

Read often and insatiably the books of the teachers of the Church on divine providence. ... Read also the two Testaments, which God ordained for knowledge of the whole world. ... To exchange one converse for another, occupy yourself with reading books which will make plain to you the subtle pathways of ascetical discipline, of contemplation, and of the lives of the saints. ... And when you stand up to pray and to say your rule of prayer, instead of thinking of what you have seen and heard in the world, you will find yourself pondering the divine Scriptures you have read. ... By reading the soul is enlightened anew and helped always to pray assiduously and without confusion.

In this sense, reading is 'the source of pure prayer'.

Yet 'not all books are profitable for the concentration of the mind'. An ascetic should abstain, above all, from reading heterodox literature: 'Beware of reading books that delineate the doctrines of creeds with a view to explaining them, for they, more than anything else, can arm the spirit of blasphemy against you'. Beyond that, any sort of literature outside the compass of scriptural and patristic writings should be excluded from the ascetic's daily reading as a potential distraction:

For the rest, any kind of reading that there may be will actually cause him loss and darken his mind, obscuring its goal, which lies with God. These other kinds of reading will bring upon him darkness and listlessness during the time of the Office and prayer.

Not only secular literature, but even the books of the Fathers on dogmatic matters are not always useful for someone whose intellect has not been cleansed of the passions. To some people only ascetical literature may be recommended:

There are also people whom not even reading about God's acts of dispensation will profit, and they get no benefit thereby. For the most part they may actually become more darkened, because they are much more in need of some reading on the topic of putting the passions aright. Everyone benefits, and progresses, as a result of the reading appropriate to the stage he has reached.

The last phrase reflects a general attitude of ancient monasticism: the only significance reading has is its improvement of one's life. A monk is not supposed to be well-read: he is rather supposed to be pure in mind. Hence Isaac's recommendation:

The course of your reading should be parallel to the aim of your way of life. ... Most books that contain instructions in doctrine are not useful for purification. The reading of many diverse books brings distraction of mind down on you. Know, then, that not every book that teaches about religion is useful for the purification of the consciousness and the concentration of the thoughts.

The recommendation to abstain not only from secular reading, but also from christian dogmatic literature may seem to be a kind of obscurantism on Isaac's part. Isaac seems, however, not to mean that a monk is not in need of understanding christian doctrine clearly and distinctly. His intention was, first, to remind his reader of a monastic maxim which is very traditional indeed: reading should correspond to life. In addition, we must remember that Isaac and his contemporaries lived in a situation of continuing christological conflict. His warning should be understood in the context of that situation: he did not want the monks to be involved in any kind of theological argument, even on questions of truth and true faith. 'Someone who has tasted the truth will not enter into dispute concerning the truth. ... He is not even aroused concerning the faith'. True faith, according to Isaac, derives not from books, but from experience: it is born of purification of mind rather than of reading.

Let us now mark Isaac's suggestions concerning how do read Scripture.

His first requirement for any kind of reading in the cell is that it be done in silence and stillness: 'Persevere in reading while dwelling in stillness that your intellect may be drawn toward the awestruck wonder at all times … Let your reading be done in stillness which nothing disturbs'.

His second requirement is collectedness of mind and the absence of exterior thoughts: 'Be free of all concern for the body and the turmoil of affairs, so that through the sweet understanding of the sense of Scripture which surpasses all the senses you may savour that most sweet taste in your soul…'

His third requirement is prayer before beginning to reading: 'Do not approach the words of the mysteries contained in the divine Scriptures without prayer and beseeching God for help, but say: "Lord, grant me to perceive the power in them!" Reckon prayer to be the key to the true understanding of the divine Scriptures'.

The understanding of the inner and hidden meaning of Scripture is the main goal of reading. This is not a question of the allegorical interpretation of the text, which was not favoured by the east-syrian tradition, even though Isaac did employ it here and there. At stake here are mystical insights (sukkale) into the spiritual meaning of certain scriptural words and phrases which appear in an ascetic's mind while reading with deep recollectedness and attention. These insights are like a ray of the sun that suddenly appears in the mind of the person who reads:

Do not … overly scrutinize words that are written from experience for nurturing your way of life and that help you, by their lofty insights, to elevate yourself. Discern the purport of all the passages that you come upon in sacred writings, so as to immerse yourself deeply therein, and to fathom the profound insights found in the compositions of enlightened men. Those who in their way of life are led by divine grace to be enlightened are always aware of something like a noetic ray running between the written lines which enables the mind to distinguish words spoken simply from those spoken with great meaning for the soul's enlightenment. When in a common way a man reads lines that contain great meaning, he makes his heart common and devoid of that holy power which gives the heart a most sweet taste through intuitions that awe the soul. Everything is wont to run to its kindred; and the soul that has a share of the Spirit, on hearing the phrase that has spiritual power hidden within, ardently draws out its content for herself. Not every man is wakened to wonder by what is said spiritually and has great power concealed in it.

This passage can serve as a summary of Isaac's understanding of Holy Scripture. He discerns in it, on the one hand, 'the words spoken simply' which say nothing to one's heart and mind, and, on the other hand, 'what is said spiritually' and what is aimed directly at the reader's soul. This distinction does not imply that there are in Scripture both meaningful and meaningless words: it suggests instead that not every word of Scripture has equal significance to each reader. Isaac puts the accent on the subjective attitude of the person reading to the text being read: there are words and phrases that leave him cool and indifferent, and there are some which enkindle the flame of the love of God in him. What is important is not to miss these 'meaningful' verses of Scripture and not to be devoid of the spiritual insights contained in them.

When an ascetic reads Scripture, striving to perceive its hidden content, his understanding increases as long as he reads, and he is led gradually to the state of spiritual wonder. Once having attained it, he is totally immersed in God. An ascetic,

Isaac tells us,

… will certainly remain unvexed by the passions if he passes his time in the study of the divine Scriptures, seeking out their meanings. For because of the understanding of the divine Scriptures which grows and abides in him, vain thoughts hastily flee from him, and his mind is unable to separate itself from its yearning and the recollection of the Scriptures. Nor will his mind be able to give any attention whatever to this life by reason of the great sweetness of the rumination by which, in the ascetic's profound stillness in the desert, it is exalted. Wherefore he even forgets himself and his nature, he becomes like a man in ecstasy who has no recollection at all of this age. With special diligence he ponders and reflects on what pertains to God's majesty, and he says, 'Glory be to his Divinity!', and again, 'Glory be to his wondrous acts!… .' And so the ascetic, engrossed in these marvels and continually struck with wonder, is always intoxicated as he lives, as it were, the life after the resurrection.

Isaac expounds his teaching on reading Scripture in Chapter XXIX of Part II, whose title is'… On the great benefits which are born from converse with the Scriptures and from the hidden ministry and the meditation and constant searching out it involves, and from the search for the subject of what it teaches. And against people who find fault with those who diligently apply themselves to this wondrous and divine labour… .' Although polemical in character, this text is not a reaction against a particular heresy, like Messalianism. Isaac is contending here against the view, which was probably widespread in monastic circles, that reading books is useless and that only active work is required of a monk.

Those who consider active work and bodily labour higher than reading are in error, Isaac asserts. To perform physical labour is 'the way and norm of secular people'. For ascetics, it is far more important that their mind be continually filled with the thought of the divine economy: this constitutes 'the complete performance and sum of our Lord's commandments'. Someone whose recollection is forever bound up with the Lord by means of reading and prayer 'has fixed in himself all the works of excellence' and 'has brought them to complete fulfillment, with nothing lacking'.

Reading, Isaac assures us, is the fountainhead of prayer. By means of reading and prayer we are transported in the direction of the love of God, whose sweetness is poured out continually in our hearts like honey in a honeycomb, and our souls exult at the taste which the hidden ministry of prayer and the reading of Scripture pour into our hearts.

By prayer and reading, as well as through love of God that is born of them, the human heart is enkindled with flame. Ascetics remain in constant converse with God, and their intellect 'causes a particular symbol of Truth to blossom forth as a result of the continual delight in the momentous words with which such people labour night and day'. The search for the spiritual meanings of the words of Scripture leads them to the state of deep inner joy:

And what more is greater than this, than that someone should be continually rejoicing in God, praising him at every moment with a new song of praise which as a result of wonder springs forth from the heart that rejoices—together with other such things as are born from this source, such as the prayer which springs forth all suddenly, continuously, and involuntarily, from the depths of the heart which has become a searcher-out of spiritual meanings.

Isaac then denounces those who read Scripture only with the aim of 'receiving from the Scriptures the material for human glory, or a sharpening of the mind'. One should read Scripture only 'for the sake of truth'; only then is one's mind

dwelling continually in heaven, making conversation with God at every moment, with his thoughts wandering in yearning for the world to come,... and his mind meditates on the hope to come, and throughout all his life he chooses no other task or labour or ministry that is greater than this one.

In this state, one becomes like the angels and reflects only on God and things divine.

All the texts quoted here show how important the reading of Scripture, and patristic literature, was to Isaac, and how integral it was to his idea of prayer. We should remember that in christian antiquity, especially in monastic practice, reading was done not simply with the eyes, but aloud, even by those who were alone. Scripture was read slowly, with pauses for reflecting on the meaning of each phrase and every word. This culture of reading has fallen practically into disuse in modern times because of the necessity of gulping great quantities of meaningless words and skimming tens and hundreds of pages. Even today, however, the 'prayerful reading' Isaac recommended— that is, reading involving keen attention of mind to every word—remains an ideal for anyone who wants to penetrate the spiritual meaning of Holy Scripture. The experience and the recommendations of Isaac have not lost their validity.

For all his love of reading, especially Scripture, Isaac admits that one can reach a spiritual state in which no reading is necessary:

Until a man has received the Comforter, he requires inscriptions in ink to imprint the memory of good in his heart, to keep his striving for good constantly renewed by continual reading, and to preserve his soul from the subtleties of the ways of sin; for he has not yet acquired the power of the Spirit that drives away the delusion which takes soul-profiting recollections captive and makes a man cold through the distraction of his intellect. When the power of the Spirit has penetrated the noetic powers of the active soul, then in place of the laws written in ink, the commandments of the Spirit take root in his heart and a man is secretly taught by the Spirit and needs no help from sensory matter.

Isaac was not alone in emphasising the priority of spiritual experience over any formal expression of this experience, even the reading of scriptural and ascetical texts. This is, in fact, one of the characteristic themes of monastic and hagiographic literature. For Isaac, the text being read is not more important than the spiritual and mystical insights which the reader receives by means of reading. Reading as a form of converse with God leads to converse in which the activity of the mind ceases as we enter into direct contact with God.

5. NIGHT PRAYER

Nocturnal prayer is traditional in christian liturgical practice in general, and in particular, in the monastic practice of prayer. When recommending night vigils to monks, teachers of the ascetical life emphasised that night is the most suitable time for prayer, because then the whole world is immersed in sleep and there is nothing to distract an ascetic. 'Let every prayer that you offer in the night', Isaac says, 'be more precious in your eyes than all your activities of the day'. Keeping night vigil is a 'work filled with delight' during which 'the soul experiences that immortal life, and by means of this experience she puts off the vesture of darkness and receives the gifts of the Spirit'.

Isaac develops the theme of nocturnal vigil in Homilies XX and LXXV of Part I. The first of them provides us with some theoretical background on the vigil; the second contains mainly practical advice, with references to the lives of the saints. The second homily in question is only partly included in the west-syrian recension of Isaac and so only some of it has been translated into Greek. First, we will look at what Isaac says about nocturnal prayer in Homily XX and then see, on the basis of Homily LXXV, how this vigil was practised in Eastern monasticism.

Homily XX begins with a 'praise of vigil', which Isaac regards as an angelic activity leading to God:

Do not imagine, O man, that among all the works of monastics there is any practice greater than night vigil. ... A monk who perseveres in vigil with a discerning intellect will seem not to be clad with flesh, for this is truly the work of the angelic estate. ... A soul which labours in the practice of vigil and excels therein will have the eyes of cherubim, that she may at all times gaze upon and espy celestial visions.

However, as Isaac immediately points out, the labour of vigil is useful only when the ascetic preserves himself during the day from distraction and worldly cares. Otherwise, while standing at the vigil, he will not be able to concentrate his mind and his whole night labour will be fruitless.

Why, O man, do you govern your life with such a lack of discernment? You stand the whole night through and suffer travail in psalmody, hymns, and supplications, and does a little heedfulness during the day seem to you to be too great and arduous a task, if thereby you are deemed worthy of God's grace granted you on account of your diligence in other works? Why do you belabour yourself, when at night you sow, but during the day you dissipate your toil which is thus rendered unfruitful? ... If, however, you had made your cultivation and the fervour of your heart's converse during the day conform to your night's meditation, and you had placed no wall of separation between them, then in a short time you would have embraced Jesus' bosom.

The person who guards himself during the day knows the power of night vigil. By itself, it can replace other virtues: '... If a man's body be enfeebled by illness and he cannot fast, vigil alone can gain for the intellect steadfastness in prayer and bestow upon his heart noetic insight to understand the nature of spiritual power'. Moreover, if someone has not the strength to make prostrations and recite psalms by reason of spiritual darkening and laxity, then vigil alone, even while sitting, will be adequate for him:

If these works [prostrations and psalmody] depart from you and you cannot perform them, at least remain wakeful in a sitting position, pray with your heart, and make every effort to pass the night without sleeping, sitting and pondering good thoughts. And if you do not harden your heart and darken it with sleep, then by the grace that first fervour, lightness and strength will return to you and you will leap with joy, giving thanks unto God.

Turning now to Isaac's Homily LXXV, let us look at his practical recommendations for keeping vigil. First, he gives advice on how to begin nocturnal prayer. One should not commence without proper preparation, which means first making a prostration, then making the sign of the Cross, standing in silence for a while, and then praying in one's own words:

When you desire to take your stand in the liturgy of your vigil, with God as your helper, do as I tell you. Bend your knees, as is the custom, but do not immediately begin your liturgy. After you have made a prayer and completed it, and signed your heart and your limbs with the life-creating sign of the cross, stand silently for a moment until your senses have been set at rest and your thoughts have become tranquil. Then raise your inner vision up to the Lord and beseech him with an afflicted soul to fortify your weakness and to grant that the psalmody of your tongue and the reflections of your heart may be pleasing to his will, saying quietly in the prayer of your heart the following: 'O Lord Jesus my God, thou who overseest thy creation, thou to whom my passions, the infirmity of our nature, and the might of our adversary are evident, do thou thyself shelter me from the wickedness of our common enemy … Do thou safeguard me from the turmoil of thoughts and the inundation of passions, and account me worthy to perform this sacred liturgy, lest perchance I should taint its sweetness by my passions and be found as one shameless and audacious before thee'.

This prayer is not taken from any liturgical rite but was composed by Isaac himself, as were many other prayers spread through his writings. Isaac highly valued praying in one's own words and recommended that a Christian not limit himself to reciting prayers prescribed by rule but find his own words for converse with God.

At the same time, the night vigil of every ascetic included a certain 'rule', that is, the succession of prayers, psalms, hymns, readings, and prostrations which were to be done every time the vigil is kept. This rule, according to Isaac, does not, however, need to contain a fixed number of prayers: to remain in God with one's intellect is much more important than to adhere rigidly to a particular rule.

It behooves us to observe our liturgy in complete freedom from every childish and disquieting thought. If we see that there is little time and that dawn will overtake us before we finish our liturgy, then let us voluntarily omit one marmita with prudence, or even two, from that which is the customary rule, lest we give place to turmoil, and obliterate the sweet taste of our liturgy… .

Precisely for this reason, one should not recite psalms hastily, with the aim of finishing the rule sooner, and so lose the savour of one's vigil.

If, while you are observing your liturgy, a thought should accost you and whisper to you, saying, 'Hasten a little, your work is multiplying; free yourself of it quickly', then pay no attention to it. But if this thought disturbs you more, immediately go back to the last marmita, or as many as you like, and chant each verse repeatedly with understanding. … And if the thought troubles you again, or straitens you, leave off your psalmody, and bend your knees in prayer, saying: 'I wish not to count up words, but to attain to heavenly mansions… .'

In Isaac's opinion, then, the first way of resisting the thoughts consists in reciting psalms slowly, repeating every verse many times, while the second, in leaving off the prescribed psalms and praying with one's own words.

If, Isaac continues, as a result of standing a long time in prayer you become feeble from fatigue and the thought intrudes, 'Finish up, for you can stand no longer', then answer: 'No, but I shall sit down, for even this is better than sleep. Although my tongue is silent and utters no psalm, yet my mind is engaged with God in prayer and in my converse with him; wakefulness is always more profitable than sleep'. Here our attention is drawn to Isaac's permission to replace reading aloud with silent prayer in one's mind. Prayer aloud was probably a common practice among the ascetics of his time; prayer in the mind was prescribed for times when one is tired, or during some common activity, when one is not alone.

Then Isaac goes on to say that the order of nocturnal vigil is not the same for all ascetics. As well as numerous means of attaining attention and humility, there are many types of vigil and various sequences of prayers that may be read. Of special interest is Isaac's reference to the prayer with a short formula and to the practice of praying without kneeling:

Neither prayer nor simple psalmody fully comprise a monk's vigil. One person continues in psalmody all the night long; another passes the night in repentance, compunctionate entreaties, and prostrations; another in weeping, tears, and lamentation over his sins. It is written concerning one of our fathers that for forty years his prayer consisted of but one saying, 'As a man I have sinned, but thou, as God, forgive me'. The fathers heard him sorrowfully meditating upon this verse, and how he wept and would not be silent. This prayer took the place of his liturgy both night and day. Another man spends part of his evening in psalmody and the rest of the night he chants songs, glorifications, hymns, and other mournful melodies. Another man passes the night in glorifying God and in reading marmyata, and between each marmita he illumines and refreshes himself with reading from the Bible until he is rested. And again another makes for himself the rule not to bend his knees, not even in the prayer that concludes a marmita, though this is customary during vigils, and he passes the entire night in unbroken silence.

This reference to Moses the Black, who prayed without kneeling, concludes Homily LXXV in the west-syrian recension and in the greek translation. In the original version follow passages in which Isaac speaks of the spiritual joy that overtakes a person during night vigil:

While the strenuous take their delight in such diverse things and their like during their vigils, they pass the entire duration of the long hours of the night without despondency. Their souls flourish and rejoice and forget the garment of flesh. … From the delight and the leaping of their hearts they do not bring sleep to mind, for they think that they have put off the body or that they have already reached that state which will be theirs after the resurrection. And because of their great joy they sometimes leave off psalmody, and they fall on their faces on account of the onrush of joy that surges in their souls. The whole length of the night is like the day to them, and the coming of darkness is like the rising of the sun by reason of that hope which exalts their hearts and inebriates them by its meditation. … While their tongue plays on the spiritual lyre, their intellect looks after its own matters. Sometimes it turns toward the sense of the verses, sometimes it repulses an alien thought as it appears, and sometimes, when the soul grows weary, the intellect turns to the contents of the reading for the day.

Then Isaac returns to recommendations for prayer in a state of fatigue. If someone wishes to give his body a little rest, he should sit down facing the East. So long as he is sitting, he should not allow his mind to be idle, but reflect upon the usefulness of night vigil and upon how the ancient Fathers persevered in this labour. From these reflections, a person is seized by wonder, thinking of the great tradition to which he is heir. Many examples of great Fathers who toiled in night vigil—Isaac gives several names—lead a person to spiritual inebriation, for it seems to him that he abides with these saints and sees them.

And by remembering the lives of the saints which his intellect conceives through recalling their histories, and by musing upon them, his despondency forthwith vanishes, sloth is put to flight, his limbs are strengthened, sleep is driven from his eyelids … and ineffable joy arises in the soul. And further, sweet tears moisten the cheeks, spiritual jubilation inebriates the intellect, the soul receives inexpressible consolations, hope supports the heart and makes it courageous. Then it seems to that man that he dwells in heaven during his vigil, which is so replete with good things.

The theme of 'spiritual inebriation' is the single most characteristic mystical theme in the works of Isaac the Syrian. In the next chapter we shall analyze it in greater detail. For the moment, let us simply point to the ecstatic character of night prayer, which, according to Isaac, is a source of supernatural joy and illumination. 'For there is nothing which makes the mind so radiant and joyous and so enlightens it and expels evil thoughts, causing the soul to exult, as do continual vigils'.

Christ himself, Isaac says, 'continually separated himself for prayer, and not indiscriminately, but he chose the night for this, and as a place, the desert'. And all the revelations given to the saints came to them mostly during their prayer at night.

Prayer offered up at night possesses great power, greater than the prayer of the daytime. Therefore all the righteous prayed during the night, while combating the heaviness of the body and the sweetness of sleep. This is why Satan fears the labour of night vigil and uses every means to prevent ascetics from doing it, as was the case with Anthony the Great, the blessed Paul, Arsenius, and other egyptian Fathers. Yet the saints diligently persevered in vigils and overcame the power of the devil. Which one of the solitaries, though possessing all the virtues together, could neglect this work, and not be reckoned idle without it? For night vigil is the light of the thinking (tar'ita); and by it the understanding (mad'a) is exalted, the mind (re'yana) is collected, and the intellect (hauna) takes flight and gazes at spiritual things and by prayer is rejuvenated and shines brightly.

This passage is unique in Isaac in that he uses together all four syriac terms relative to the mental faculties of the human person. By doing so, Isaac probably wants to emphasize that night prayer can embrace an entire person and totally transfigure the person's whole intellectual sphere. Nocturnal prayer has, in Isaac, an all-embracing character and is regarded as a universal means for attaining illumination of mind. The favourite hero of Isaac, Saint Arsenius, 'on the eve of the Lord's day [i.e. Sunday] would leave the sun behind his back and stretch out his hands toward heaven, until the sun rose and shone in his face'. By constant vigils, Arsenius reached a state of such illumination that his entire body became like flame when he prayed. In the same manner Saint Pachomius, who was equal to Arsenius, kept vigil and became pure in heart to such an extent that 'he saw God, who is invisible, as it were in a mirror'. 'These are the fruits of vigil,' Isaac emphasizes, 'these are the blessings of its practitioners, and these are the crowns of its struggle'.

Transfiguration of the mind, purification of the heart, and mystical vision of God are the fruits of night vigil. Isaac concludes by appealing to his reader to imitate the ancient saints in order to become 'a partaker of these saints and a heir to their way of life'.

6. THE 'RULE OF SLAVERY' AND THE 'RULE OF FREEDOM'

Isaac, as we saw, prescribes that nocturnal prayer should be performed 'in complete freedom' from the childish wish to adhere to a prescribed rule. He constantly returns to this prescription, emphasizing that a 'slavish' attitude, by which reciting the required number of prayers is regarded as the most important thing, does not liberate one from confusion or outside thoughts; 'freedom', on the other hand, brings about a peaceful state of mind and soul:

Do you wish to take delight in the psalmody of your liturgy and to understand the oracles of the Spirit which you recite? Then disregard completely the quantity of verses, and set at naught your skill in giving rhythm to the verses, so that you may speak them in the manner of a prayer. Abandon your customary repetition by heart, and understand what I tell you. ... And when your mind is made steadfast in these meditations, then confusion will give place and depart from you. Peace of thought is not to be found in slavish activity; nor in the freedom of the children of God is there found the confusion and turmoil.

In Chapter IV of Part II, Isaac teaches that the rule, which includes many different prayers, is suitable for those whose minds have not yet reached the state of illumination, whereas the illumined mind needs no such rule. Similarily, a rule is useful in the state of spiritual laxity but needless during periods of grace.

A mind which has once been illumined has no need of the varied wording of various prayers: just the single door of prayer suffices to enfold the mind within prayer, allowing it to mingle with God. Varieties of prayers indeed greatly help a mind which is harassed by distraction: by them, and by means of the strength resulting from them, the mind experiences compunction and so acquires sweet prayer, prolonged kneeling, intercession for creation, and extended supplications which are set into motion from within. This happens to someone because, with each single word which he encounters in these prayers, he is like someone who is wakened from sleep: he encounters in them astounding insights all the time, seeing that these very words are the result of the gift of grace and so possess a hidden power. ... During periods of grace, when you enjoy this prayer of delight and those prolonged kneelings, there is no great need for you to stand by the canonical Hours or to worry yourself over the matter of the number of prayers that remain to be recited, for such prayer has encompassed within itself prayers which are recited according to fixed number and it has made the canons subordinate to you.

Pure prayer, Isaac continues, is the pinnacle of the work of prayer: someone who has attained to it has no need of canonical rules. Anyone who has not attained pure prayer, however, should not abandon rules. If someone partially possesses pure prayer, then he should 'keep the canonical rule for the other part'. Keeping rules is necessary during one's spiritual childhood; but when one has reached maturity, rules become ineffective. There is 'the law of children which brings the person up in freedom and gives him light', and there is 'the law of servants which does not allow progress, and whereby a person is educated in a way befitting young children'. The first corresponds to the 'rule of freedom'; it is the attitude a son has towards a father and does not require special rules; the second corresponds to the 'rule of slavery' and needs canonical boundaries. As long as someone prays only at specific times of day, he should observe the canonical offices; but if he is able to pray unceasingly, lying prostrate before the cross, then he is not subject to any law or canonical rules, nor do times and specific appointed periods have any authority over him; rather, he is from that point on above them, being with God without any limitation.

Isaac develops the same theme, but in an entirely different context, in the anti-messalian Chapter XIV of Part II, of which we have already spoken. Here the accent is laid on the utility and necessity of the rule of prayer, which is contrasted to the messalian denial of external forms of prayer. Even here, however, Isaac describes those states in which one can neglect the rule of prayer in the delight which comes from the divine love:

The following is a bad sign when it appears: that someone should neglect the duty of the Hours of the Office without any pressing reasons. But if it is prayer which has drawn someone to neglect these Hours, and if it is the compulsion and weighty experience of long drawn out prayer which has led him to desist from them, or if the delay brought about by prayer's overpowering delight causes him to neglect the time of Office, then this person has chanced upon a splendid piece of merchandise as a result of the change brought about by the enviable object which has fallen into his hands. ... All is well, provided he does not neglect the time of the Office as a result of empty ideas or a contemptuous attitude, but rather the sweet delight found in prayer has held him fast, as a result of the constraint of divine love—for this, after all, is the fulfillment of our ministry, and is not constrained by, or subject to, any rule.

Isaac alternates, as it were, between criticism of the Messalians' 'contemptuous attitude' to rule and his own conviction that observing rules is not always necessary and not always possible for an Orthodox ascetic. He obviously did not want his own love of freedom to be confused with Messalianism, and therefore very decisively dissociated himself from it by emphasizing that in Orthodox tradition abandoning rules results, not from contempt and arrogance, but rather from the abundance of the love of God which forces the person praying sometimes to forget rules entirely.

And if such things occur to someone continually—and they are a sign of divine charisms and a mighty opening to purity of prayer—and especially if he manifests a reverential outward posture and profound reverence during his prayer, then that person is quickly raised to the rank of the perfected. But if someone decides to abandon what belongs first of all, without yet having found what comes afterwards, then it is clear that he is being mocked by the demons... .

The rule is useful, Isaac claims, because it teaches humility, whereas neglecting the rule may lead one to pride:

The heart acquires greater freedom of speech with God during prayer than it does during the Office. But complete neglect of the Office causes pride, and it is out of pride that one falls away from God. You see, the very fact that someone forces himself to be subjected to a rule—when he is quite free in his way of life—keeps the soul humble, and offers no opportunity for the demon of pride to dangle before him some evil thought. By continually considering himself as insignificant and not capable of freedom, he humbles and brings low any pride of thought. There is no more effective bridle than this to place in the mouth of the mind that exalts itself.

Precisely for this reason the ancient Fathers did not abandon their rule, even though they possessed unceasing prayer:

It was not to no purpose that these Fathers imposed upon themselves, in some cases one hundred, in others fifty or sixty or more, prayers—even though they had already entirely become an altar of prayer. Why were fixed numbers so necessary, when they never ceased from prayer? It is said that Evagrius had one hundred, the blessed Macarius sixty, and Moses the Black, the Ethiopian, had fifty, whereas a certain great solitary, Paul, had three hundred, and so on. The reason why these blessed Fathers compelled themselves, like servants, to keep such rules was fear of pride.

A rule induces in the soul the humility that belongs to servitude. Yet in the rule itself, there is liberty, as in liberty there is a rule. Some people make progress as a result of rule; and some as a result of the liberty which comes from it.

In freedom someone makes more progress than when subject to a rule. Nevertheless, often enough out of freedom there spring up many paths leading to error; in freedom there lurk many varieties of downfall. Whereas with a rule no one ever goes astray; those who persevere under the yoke of some rule will only be driven to some downfall once they have abandoned that rule and disregarded it. For this reason the saints of old who completed their course without going astray, governed themselves by means of some rule.

According to Isaac, 'there is a rule involving liberty and there is a rule for slaves'. The latter consists of reciting a fixed number of psalms and prayers at every Office. The person who is subject to this rule,… is inalterably bound by obligation, without the possibility of change, to these same psalms all his days—all because he is tied to the obligation, in prayer and in the Office, to follow the details of the number, length, and fixed character of their quantity which he has decreed and fixed for himself. All this is utterly alien to the path of true knowledge, for such a person does not bear in mind either divine activity or the feebleness of nature, or the hazard of frequent battles: in the first case grace may be given so that he tarries beyond what his will has decreed; in the second case human nature may prove too weak to fulfill the rule. …

In other words, someone who appoints for himself a fixed quantity of prayers to be recited at certain hours of the day does not take into account that he may be incapable of observing these rules, either out of the abundance of grace which forces him to forget the words of prayer, or out of physical weakness which saps him of the strength to recite the prescribed prayers.

The 'rule of liberty', on the contrary, does not fix the sequence and number of prayers to be said. Each monk should maintain the traditional seven times of prayer during the day, but the content and length of these Hours are left to discretion:

The rule of liberty consists in one's unfailing observance of the seven Offices, ordained for our chaste mode of life by Holy Church at the hands of the Fathers who were assembled by the Holy Spirit for the ecumenical synod. Far be it from us solitaries that we not be subject to the Church or her leaders or laws. This is precisely the reason why we observe the ordinance of the seven Hours of the Office, in conformity with what the Church has laid down for us, as her children. This does not mean, however, that for each Office I should perform the same particular fixed number of psalms; nor does one fix each day a particular number of prayers to be said between these Offices, during both night and day. And one does not set a time limit for each of these prayers, nor does one decide upon specific words to use. Rather, one spends as long on each prayer as grace provides the strength, asking whatever the pressing need of the moment may require, using whatever prayer one is stirred to use. And while such a person prays he is all the more recollected and undistracted in view of the delight of this kind of prayer. During such prayers a person measures his request in conformity with the strength of human nature and the wisdom that the Lord accords to him.

This passage, by emphasising that monks are to be obedient to the Church, again constitutes an attack upon the Messalians who reject the tradition of the Church in advocating spontaneous prayer. At the same time, the seven times of prayer are presented as a framework for monastic prayer, which can also be somewhat spontaneous: neither the sequence of prayers nor their length is fixed. Among the factors which influence the length and sequence of prayer are 'the pressing need of the moment' or 'the strength of nature'. In other words, prayer should not ignore the needs of the person who prays and it should not by its length exceed the person's natural limitations.

As to the words to be recited, none of the written prayers, not even the Lord's Prayer is compulsory, according to Isaac. The importance of even this prayer is not restricted to its words; what is important is that the one who prays it is penetrated by its spirit:

If someone says that in all our prayers we should recite the prayer uttered by our Saviour, using the same wording and keeping the exact order of the words rather than their sense, such a person is very deficient in his understanding of our Saviour's purpose in uttering this prayer, nor has he ever drawn close to the thinking of the Blessed Interpreter. Our Lord did not teach us a particular sequence of words here; rather, the teaching he provided in this prayer consists in showing us on what we should be focusing our minds during the entire course of our life. It was the sense that he gave us, and not the precise sequence of words to be recited by our lips. Thus, whenever we set this prayer before our minds as something to aim at, we will pray following its sense, and we will direct the movements of our own prayer in accordance with it, as we ask for the kingdom and righteousness, or, as may sometimes be the case, for escape from temptations; and at times we may be asking for the needs of our human nature, that is, for sustenance for the day; likewise with all the other things, in accordance with the aims with which he provided us, telling us what we should pray for. So our prayer should be inspired by its sense, and we should set aright our lives in strict accordance with it. ...

When our Lord gave this prayer to his disciples, he was concerned, not with the sequence and order of words, but with instructing the disciples 'not to intermingle into prayer, as do the pagans, all sorts of other things which are contrary to his commandments'. To think otherwise reflects... a childish mentality which investigates and is concerned with the exact sequence of words rather than with setting its sight on their sense, out of which spring prayers, requests, and reflections excellently suited to the conduct of the New World. Altering the outward form of the words of the prayer which our Lord handed down makes no difference provided our prayer stems from its sense, and that the mind follows that sense.

These passages make clear that Isaac was in favour of a free attitude to the rule of prayer and to the texts to be used in one's rule. What is important is that prayer should correspond to the inner need of the person who prays and to Jesus Christ's teaching on prayer. One can pray in one's own words and can use the psalms and prayers written by others: in the latter case the words that originally belonged to another person should become the words of the person who prays them, that is, they should pass through the depths of his own heart. Faithfulness to Christ consists not in the literal repetition of the prayer he gave, but in being imbued with its spirit. In the same manner, faithfulness to the Church and the monastic tradition consists not in reciting all the Offices and psalms written by the ancient Fathers, but in being filled with the spirit of those Fathers and in attaining to the measure of their sanctity.

7. PRAYER FOR THE WORLD

Isaac the Syrian was one of those ancient Church writers who possessed a universal vision encompassing a constant memory of the entire world and the whole creation, of all people and their sufferings. This is the paradox of a solitary life: withdrawing from people, a recluse does not forget them; renouncing the world, he does not cease praying for it. Isaac loved solitude and stillness, but any kind of closing in upon himself, any thought of his own salvation apart from his brethren, was entirely alien to him. He possessed that 'merciful heart' which is characterized by having compassion on all creatures, not only Christians, but also apostates, animals, and demons. His personal prayer, like liturgical prayer, grew to a cosmic scale, embracing not only neighbours and strangers, but the whole of humanity and the entire universe.

This exceptional experience of universal prayer can be seen in a lengthy prayer for the whole world which is contained in Chapter V of Part II. Isaac begins by giving thanks to God for his Incarnation:

As my soul bows down to the ground I offer you with all my bones and all my heart the worship that befits you. O glorious God, who dwells in ineffable silence. You have built for my renewal a tabernacle of love on earth where it is your good pleasure to rest, a temple made of flesh and fashioned with the most holy sanctuary oil. Then you filled it with your holy presence so that all worship might be fulfilled in it, indicating the worship of the eternal Persons of your Trinity and revealing to the worlds which in your grace you created an ineffable mystery, a power which cannot be felt or grasped by any part of your creation which has come into being. In wonder at it angelic beings are plunged into silence, awed at the dark cloud of this eternal mystery and at the flood of glory which issues from within the source of wonder, for it receives worship in the sphere of silence from every intelligence that has been sanctified and made worthy of you.

Our attention is drawn by the language of the opening petitions, which is very close to that of the psalms: such phrases as 'with all my bones and with all my heart' are clearly inspired by the images of the psalter. Continuing his prayer, Isaac turns his mind to the creation and the fall of man, projecting the latter upon himself. Isaac speaks of himself as a child and implores God to treat him with fatherly care:

I prostrate myself, Lord, at the footstool of your feet and at your holy right hand which has fashioned and made me a human being capable of becoming aware of you. But I have sinned and done wrong, both in myself and before you, for I have abandoned holy converse with you and have given my days over to converse with the lusts. I beg of you, Lord, do not set against me the sins of my youth, the ignorance of my old age, and the frailty of my nature … Rather, turn my heart towards you, away from the troublesome distraction of the lusts; cause to dwell within me a hidden light. Your acts of goodness towards me always anticipate any kind of volition on my part to do well and any readiness for virtue on the part of my heart. You have never held back your care to test my freewill; rather, as with the care of a father towards his young son, so has your care for me run after me,… for you knew all the time that, even less than a child do I know whither I am traveling.

After requesting deliverance from evil intentions, carnal desire, and the power of the devil, Isaac asks God to give him true repentance that he may see his own sins:

At the door of your compassion do I knock, Lord. Send aid to my scattered impulses, which are intoxicated with the multitude of the passions and the power of darkness. You can see my sores hidden within me: stir up contrition—though not corresponding to the weight of my sins, for if I receive full awareness of the extent of my sins, Lord, my soul would be consumed with the bitter pain from them. … O name of Jesus, key to all gifts, open up for me the great door to your treasure-house, that I may enter and praise you with the praise that comes from the heart in return for your mercies which I have experienced in latter days; for you came and renewed me with an awareness of the New World.

Other entreaties of a rather personal character follow. Various feelings and expressions of repentance are intermingled with glorifications and praises.

Turning again to the Incarnation of God the Word, Isaac asks God to hold him worthy of insight 'into the mystery of the killing' of his beloved Son. The remembrance of Christ's death on the cross gives rise to a hymn of thanksgiving in which his prayer reaches a dramatic tension:

You have given your entire treasure to the world. … Truly this mystery is vast. … The flood of Christ's mysteries presses upon my mind like the waves of the sea. I wanted to be silent before them, and not speak, but they proved to be like burning fire that was kindled in my bones. My mind rebukes me, revealing my sins to me. Your mystery stupefies me, but urges me on to behold it. … O my Hope, pour into my heart the inebriation which consists in the hope of you. O Jesus Christ, the resurrection and light of all worlds, place upon my soul's head the crown of knowledge of you; open before me all of a sudden the door of mercies, cause the rays of your grace to shine out in my heart… .

After a long and expressive prayer to Christ in which his life and suffering for the sake of humankind are remembered, Isaac turns to prayer for monks and solitaries, both living and departed. His prayer takes on that universal ring characteristic of the eucharistic anaphoras of the Eastern Church. It is not by mere chance that he refers in his prayer to the offering of the Body and Blood of Christ:

May there be remembered, Lord, on your holy altar at that fearful moment when your Body and your Blood are sacrificed for the salvation of the world, all the fathers and brethren who are on mountains, in caves, in ravines, cliffs, rugged and desolate places, who are hidden from the world and it is only known to you where they are. … O King of all worlds and of all the Orthodox Fathers who, for the sake of the truth of the faith, have endured exile and afflictions at the hands of persecutors, who in monasteries, convents, deserts and the habitations of the world, everywhere and in every place, have made it their care to please you with labours for the sake of virtue: accompany them with Your assistance, Lord, and … may the power of your Trinity dwell in them… .

After the prayer for monks and solitaries follows one for the sick and captives:

May those who suffer from dire and grievous illnesses of the body also be remembered before you; send to them an angel of compassion and assuage their souls, which are grievously tormented by their bodies' terrible afflictions. Have pity, too, Lord, on those who are subjected to the hands of evil, wicked, and godless men; send to them speedily an angel of compassion, and save them from their plight. O my Lord and my God, send comfort to all those who are constrained by whatever kind of hardship.

In this petition, and even more in those which follow, one discerns literal parallels between Isaac's language and that of the eucharistic prayers of the Eastern Church. Thus, the prayer for deliverance of the Church from persecution and inner conflicts, and for the preservation of love and unanimity between kings and priests—i.e. between the state and the Church—reads as follows:

Lord, overshadow your holy Church which has been redeemed by your blood; cause to dwell in it your true peace which you gave to your holy apostles; bind her children in holy bonds of indissoluble love; may the rebel not have power over her, and keep far from her persecution, tumult, and wars, both from those within and from those without; and may kings and priests be bound together in great peace and love, their minds always filled with gazing towards you; and may the holy faith be a wall for your flock.

Let us recall, for comparison, a eucharistic prayer from the east-syrian Anaphora of Mar Theodore of Mopsuestia:

Lord, mighty God, accept this offering … for all kings, priests and authorities … for the whole Catholic Church, that you may cause to dwell within her your tranquillity and your peace all the days of the world. … And may persecutions, disturbances, controversies, schisms and divisions be put far away from her. And may we all be united with one another in one accord with pure heart and entire love.

In his concluding petitions, Isaac remembers those who have gone astray and those who departed this life without repentance and true faith:

I beg and beseech you, Lord: grant to all who have gone astray a true knowledge of you, so that each and every one may come to know your glory. In the case of those who have passed from this world lacking a virtuous life and having had no faith, be an advocate for them, Lord, for the sake of the body which you took from them, so that from the single united body of the world we may offer up praise to Father, Son, and Holy Spirit in the kingdom of heaven, an unending source of eternal delight.

This last petition for those who died without having true faith shows that the idea of the impossibility of prayer for the departed non-Christians was totally alien to Isaac. He did not imagine a kingdom of heaven which would be accessible only to certain chosen people while the rest of humankind remained outside it. As we can see, Isaac regards the whole world as 'a single united body' of which every human being is a member. In the age to come, the whole universe must be transformed into the Body of Christ, which is the Church of those redeemed by him. In Chapter VIII, when we discuss Isaac's eschatology, we shall see how this universal vision influences Isaac's thinking on universal salvation.

Isaac is convinced that Christians should pray for all persons, regardless of their virtues or beliefs:

We should pray with suffering, and we should make supplication to God for all these things with pain. And this is the attitude we should have towards all human beings: we should pray for them with suffering, as for ourselves, for in this way the Divinity will come and rest in us, and cause his will to reside in us 'as in heaven, so on earth'.

8. MEDITATION ON GOD AND PURE PRAYER

Among the kinds of prayer mentioned by Isaac, meditation occupies a special place. He uses several terms to designate this type of prayer, including three which are characteristic of the whole east-syrian tradition: herga, meditation; renya, reflection; 'uhdana, recollection, remembrance. Each of these three terms, for all their differences in nuance, may refer to meditation on God and on spiritual things. In this section, we shall speak principally about what Isaac called herga db-alaha, meditation on God. This mediation is closely connected with prayer, and we cannot easily separate the one from the other: prayer sometimes gives birth to meditation, and at other times it is born from meditation.

In one of his 'Gnostic Chapters', Isaac explains in detail what the practice of 'meditation on God' entails:

When you sit down between one Office and another to apply your intellect to meditation on God, add these considerations: consider how it was from complete non-existence that you came to existence; who it was who so made you that you came into being, into your present state of existence out of not existing at all; and, to speak in the terms of Scripture, how, although you were initially created beautiful, of your own will you came to be in a bad way in that you ate of the forbidden tree, and you continue to eat of it each day; and how you turned aside to evil. ... Again, consider what you have become through your own will, and in what state you are now, without any expectations, yet to what hope you have all suddenly been called by the abundance of the compassion of him who called you in Christ Jesus our Lord, returning you to your original luminous relationship with God; and how you remained in your disobedience and persisted in your fallen state, yet God did not neglect you, but of his own accord devised these excellent things for you, coming to save you when you did not even know to ask this for yourself. Again, consider what you are now in this life here, and what you are going to be after a little while; and in what state of corruption your present condition will end up, and that out of your present existence you will again become as though you had never existed—without remembrance, or name, or memorial throughout all the generations to come of this world. How can I describe what is so astonishing: that out of such a condition of corruption there should be such a new state of existence, moving from such a hovel to such an abode; and further, the comparison of what is here with what is beyond, and the transition from our present mode of life to the future life, as we move from suppositions to certain knowledge and vision.

Meditation on God presupposes remembrance of the whole economy of God concerning humanity, beginning with the creation of man, including the Incarnation and finishing with the life of the age to come. At the same time, meditation on God also includes pondering upon the ascetical life and christian virtues, as Isaac shows in Chapter X of

Part II. This meditation, according to Isaac, leads to spiritual illumination:

Everyone, then, will find illumination in that meditation into which he throws himself and in the reflection he examines assiduously in his mind: by it he will gain wisdom and will concentrate more on it if, in reflecting on the ministry of righteousness, he ponders the actions of righteousness, and he will be illumined. ... And if, again, he reflects on the ministry of virtue—how he can please God in the purity of his body, the toil of prayer, the clarifying of his body through fasting, the recitation of psalmody, and the struggle against all the things that hinder these; and if he reflects on how many different forms virtue divides itself up into—and through which of its constituent parts he finds illumination and advances while persevering particularly in it—and reflects on what is standing in opposition to each of these, then he will thereby grow deep in understanding.

This examination of virtues and their various kinds, which Isaac suggests, is a meditation on moral issues. It is necessary for an ascetic to practise it, as it provides a theoretical background for a virtuous life. But it is important that one reflect not only on the negative aspect of the ascetical life—that is, the struggle against the passions and thoughts, a useful type of meditation, but far less profitable than meditation on the positive aspects of christian life:

If a person meditates on the passions, on thoughts and their struggles, on how thoughts attach themselves to one another, and on which passion is attached to which, and on what is the beginning of the first and what is the end; and on what potency each of the passions possesses and by what it is mitigated, and whence it receives potency—such a person is concentrating just on matters of the passions, exercising his intellect on them. But if he meditates on God and allows his mind to wander on the things that belong to him, searching God out single-mindedly, then he will be illumined and will encompass those former matters as well. Those former matters are fine, but they involve contests, and reflection and knowledge of soul and body should not rest all with them; nor should reflection that consists only in opposing the passions ... constitute the goal of the hope that has been preached to us. Nor is it what the Apostle said about 'attaining, with all the saints, to what is the height and depth, length and breadth', or 'Let a person excel in every kind of wisdom, and in every kind of spiritual insight'. How can he grow wise and become aware of these things if he remains night and day only with release from and arguments against passionate thoughts and continual concern for them? Nevertheless many people exercise themselves and concentrate on these—and their service is fine and arduous, but they are not in the slightest concerned with this other aspect.

Someone who is consumed by thinking about the passions and virtues is always involved in struggles: sometimes he gains victories in the spiritual life, but not infrequently is he defeated. But someone who is concerned with meditation on God finds himself above struggles against the passions:

It is not that his intellect actually vanquishes thoughts, stirrings, and passions, but it reigns over them, and they vanish away. They are not actually defeated, for no victory is involved there. Rather, the passions, memories, and all that they induce, are no longer there, for that person has actually been raised from the world, leaving behind, below where they belong, all reflection on it, its affairs in all their various sorts, and knowledge of them, while the intellect is taken from their midst. ... Once someone meditates on God and on the riches of the waves of everything that belongs to Him and applies to Him, then he has departed from the world, and the door is held closed on all memories of it, the passions remaining idle in their own places, while that person has actually been raised up from where they are.

Meditation on God, accompanied by total forgetfulness of this world, leads one to the state of spiritual contemplation in which one penetrates into the 'dark cloud' of God's glory, and becomes like the angels:

… meditating on God first stirs in a person, and then gradually meditating encompasses his intellect little by little, and it brings the intellect in and makes it stand in the dark cloud of His glory, and in that Fountain of Life whence life bursts forth at all times without interruption for the benefit of all intellects, both those above and those below— of those whose labour is set in the heights above the body and of those whose labour is on earth and dies; of those whose movements are 'burning fire' and of those whose movements are limited by their gross nature.

'Luminous meditation' on God is one of the highest stages of prayer: beyond it remains only one step to mystical 'wonder', a state in which the intellect is totally withdrawn from this world and entirely captivated by God.

If you are desirous of tasting the love of God, my brother, ponder, and with understanding meditate, on the things that pertain to him and which have to do with him and his holy nature: meditate and ponder mentally, cause your intellect to wander on this all your time, and by this you will become aware of how all the parts of your soul become enflamed with love, as a burning flame alights on your heart, and desire for God excels in you. … Luminous meditation on God is the goal of prayer; or rather, it is the fountainhead of prayers, in that prayer itself ends in reflection on God. There are times when a person is transported from prayer to a wondrous meditation on God. And there are times when prayer is born out of meditating on God. All these are different stages in the course run, in divine fashion, by the intellect in the stadium of this world, each person having his gaze fixed on the crown. The crown of the solitary is the spiritual enjoyment of Christ our Lord. Whoever has found this, has received from this world a pledge of those things which are to come.

The mutual connection between prayer and meditation is discussed in Chapter XV of Part II. 'Pure prayer' (ḥlota dkita) is the main subject of this chapter. According to Isaac, 'pure prayer' consists in 'meditation on virtue'. One should not think, suggests Isaac, that pure prayer is the complete absence of thoughts; it is instead a 'wandering' (pehya) of mind on things divine:

Purity of prayer, O disciple of truth, and the recollection of mind that exists in it consists in the exact reflection on virtue in which we carefully engage at the time of prayer. Just as purity of heart, to which the Fathers diligently exhort us, is not a matter of being totally without thought or reflection or stirring. Rather, it consists in the heart purified of all evil, and in gazing favourably on everything, and considering it from God's point of view. It is the same with pure and undistracted prayer. This does not mean that the mind is entirely devoid of any thought or wandering of any kind, but that it does not wander about on empty subjects during the time of prayer. It is not the case that the mind is outside of purity of prayer unless it is wandering about in something specifically good; it may also ponder on things that are appropriate and think thoughts pleasing to God during the time of prayer. Nor is it required of anyone that empty recollections not come at all during prayer, but one should not occupy himself with them and be distracted by them.

There are two kinds of wandering of mind: bad and good. Even pure prayer involves wandering, but it is an 'excellent wandering', as the mind is concentrated on good and divine things.

Wandering is bad when someone is distracted by empty thoughts or by reflecting on something bad, and so he thinks evil thoughts when he is at prayer before God. Wandering is good when the mind wanders on God during the entire extent of its prayer, on his glory and majesty, a wandering stemming from a recollection of the Scriptures and prompted by insights into the divine utterances and the holy words of the Spirit. ... We do not consider as alien to purity of prayer or as detrimental to collectedness of thoughts in prayer any profitable recollections that may spring up in the mind from the Writings of the Spirit, and that may result in insights and spiritual understanding of the divine world during the time of prayer. For someone to examine and think in a recollected manner about the object of his supplication and the request of his prayer is an excellent kind of prayer, provided it is consonant with the intention of our Lord's commandments. This kind of collectedness of mind is very good.

Meditation on divine things and pure prayer are thus synonymous. Isaac goes so far as to state that wandering of mind can be better than prayer if it is accompanied by insights into spiritual reality:

If the mind is released from this prayer and becomes diffused in things divine, or if there occurs to it some excellent reflection arising out of Scripture's insights on God— insights that are either individual to the person or belong to the whole community, insights into God's dispensations and acts of providence, whether they be those belonging to each successive day or universal ones—all things by which the depth of the heart is stirred to the praise of God or to thanksgiving and joy at the immensity and exalted nature of his compassion and love towards us; if this happens, this kind of wandering is even better than prayer! However exalted and pure someone's supplication may be, this is the culmination of every kind of collectedness of mind and of excellence of prayer.

'Insights' (sukkale) is one of Isaac's favourite terms: we shall return to this in the next chapter. Here we simply point out that the question concerns mystical contiguities and encounters which happen during prayer, encounters with another reality surpassing human understanding and words. Insights can be both personal and 'belonging to the community'. What might the latter entail? This concerns, not the experience of a group of people who simultaneously receive the same insight, but the personal insight of one particular member of the community into the experience of the whole Church, an insight which lets the experience of the Church become his own experience. In other words, during his prayer something is revealed to a person that was earlier revealed to other members of the Church community: by this personal revelation, the experience of the community is integrated into the experience of the particular believer. Pure prayer, therefore, allows the convergence and the unity of a single person with an ecclesiastical community and with the tradition of the Church.

Pure prayer, in Isaac's understanding, is the final aim and the highest limit of any prayer; beyond it, prayer ceases:

Even as the whole force of the laws and the commandments given by God to humankind terminate in purity of the heart, according to the word of the Fathers, so all the modes and forms of prayer by which men pray to God terminate in pure prayer. For sighs, prostrations, heart-felt supplications, sweet cries of lamentation, and all the other forms of prayer have their limitation, as I have said, and the extent of their domain in pure prayer. But once the mind crosses this boundary,… it no longer possesses prayer, or movement, or weeping, or dominion, or free will, or supplication, or desire, or fervent longing for things hoped for in this life or in the age to come. Therefore, there exists no prayer beyond pure prayer.

Those who attain purity of prayer are very rare, Isaac adds: 'Only one man among thousands will be found who … has been accounted worthy to attain to pure prayer. … But as to that mystery which is after pure prayer and lies beyond it, there is scarcely to be found a single man from generation to generation who by God's grace has attained to this knowledge'.

Pure prayer, then, is the mind wandering on divine things, when nothing earthly or vain is mingled with the stirrings of prayer. This prayer is very like meditation, and both constitute the highest stages of the labour of prayer. What is beyond the boundary of pure prayer—the so-called 'spiritual prayer', wonder, contemplation—is no longer prayer. It is that fullness of life in God which belongs to the life of the age to come: it grows out of the experience of prayer, but goes far beyond its limits.

CHAPTER VII

THE LIFE IN GOD

O man, pay attention to what you read here. Indeed, can these things be known from writings in ink? Or can the taste of honey pass over the palate by reading books? For if you do not strive, you will not find.

I/4 *(39) = PR* **4** *(58–59)*

THIS CHAPTER DEVOTED TO THE MYSTICISM of Isaac begins with the theme of 'spiritual prayer', a state in which the intellect becomes silent. Then we turn to his teaching on contemplation (theoria), 'overshadowing', and illumination. The characteristic themes of mystical 'wonder' (ecstasy) and 'inebriation' by the love of God will also be considered. Finally, we shall conclude our survey of mystical themes in Isaac with an analysis of his gnoseology, that is, his teaching on the knowledge that is born of faith in God. All these themes are closely linked and intermingled in Isaac, and it is difficult to single them out and to subject each to systematic analysis.

To give the mystical theology of Isaac the appearance of a coherent system, we need to analyze his mystical terminology. We shall therefore treat the main terms he uses to designate one or another aspect of the mystical experience. This should help us draw general conclusions concerning the character of the mysticism of Isaac the Syrian.

1. 'SPIRITUAL PRAYER' AND THE STILLNESS OF MIND

Isaac speaks of both pure prayer and 'spiritual prayer' (ḥlota ruhanayta): the latter phrase, which he borrowed from John of Apamea and other early ascetical writers, he understood as the state which is beyond the borders of pure prayer. The difference between pure prayer and the beyond-state, according to Isaac, is that, during pure prayer, one's mind is full of varied movements (zaw'e, stirrings), such as prayers for deliverance from trials, whereas in the beyond-state, the mind is free from all movements. The purity of prayer, according to him, means that the mind, when offering the movements of prayers, is not commingled with foreign thoughts and does not wander astray. 'Spiritual prayer' does not involve any movement of the mind. For

the saints of the age to come do not pray with prayer when their intellects have been swallowed up by the Spirit, but rather with awestruck wonder they dwell in that gladdening glory. So it is with us, at the time when the intellect is deemed worthy to perceive the future blessedness, it forgets itself and all things of the world, and no longer has movement with regard to any thing.

'Spiritual prayer' begins beyond the borders of pure prayer. It marks the descent of mind to a state of peace and stillness. In this state, every prayer ceases:

In the life of the spirit ... there is no longer any prayer. Every kind of prayer that exists consists on the level of the soul of beauteous thoughts which arise in a person. ... On the level and in the life of the spirit, there are no thoughts, no stirrings; no, not even any sensation or the slightest movement of the soul concerning anything, for human nature completely departs from these things and from all that belongs to itself. Instead it remains in a certain ineffable and inexplicable silence, for the working of the Holy Spirit stirs in it, having been raised above the realm of the soul's understanding.

'Stillness' (šelya) and 'spiritual prayer' are synonymous for Isaac. The state of stillness of mind is not acquired by human effort but is a gift:

When the mind is entirely without any kind of reflection, this is silence of the mind and not purity of prayer. It is one thing to pray purely, and quite another for the mind to be silent from any wandering at all or from insight into the words of prayer, and to remain without any stirring. No one is so stupid as to want to find this by means of struggle and the strength of his own will, for this is the gift of the revelation to the intellect, and it is not within the reach of pure prayer, or a matter of the will.

The term 'spiritual prayer', according to Isaac, is used by ascetical writers conditionally, as it designates the state which in the literal sense is not a prayer at all:

Sometimes spiritual prayer is called by some theoria—contemplation—and by others knowledge, and again by others the revelation of noetic things. Do you see how the Fathers interchange applications for spiritual things? For the exactitude of designations remains valid for things here, whereas there is no perfect or true name at all for things of the age to come; it is a simple state of knowing only, surpassing every appellation, every rudimentary element, form, colour, shape, and composite denomination. For this reason the Fathers employ whatever appellations they please to indicate that state of knowing once the soul's knowledge is raised out of the visible world, since no one knows its name with exactness. But so as to make the soul's deliberations steadfast therein the Fathers resort to appellations and parables, according to Saint Dionysius, who writes: 'We use parables and syllables, and permissible names, and words on account of our senses; but when our soul is moved by the operation of the Spirit toward those divine things, then both our senses and their operations are superfluous once the soul has become like unto the Godhead by an incomprehensible union, and is illumined in her movements by the ray of the sublime Light'.

Is that complete cessation of intellectual activity which Isaac calls 'stillness of mind' a migration beyond the borders of personal existence, a complete loss of personal self-awareness? No. In Isaac, 'stillness of mind' is not a synonym for unconscious and insensible oblivion: there is a positive element in Isaac's 'stillness', the capture of the mind by God. 'Stillness of mind' is a state of extremely intense activity of the mind, which finds itself entirely under the power of God and is drawn into undiscovered depths of the Spirit:

Once the intellect enters the realm of stillness, it ceases from prayer. ... As soon as the governance and the stewardship of the Spirit rule the intellect,... then a man's nature is deprived of its free will and is led by another guidance, and does not direct itself. Where, then, will prayer be, when a man's nature has no authority over itself, but is led whither it knows not by some other power, and is not able to direct the movements of the mind in what it chooses, but at that moment is held fast in a captivity by which it is guided whither it does not perceive? But according to the testimony of Scripture, at such a time a man will not possess a will, nor will he know whether he is 'in the body or out of the body'.

The state of stillness involves, therefore, the absence of the movements and desires of the intellect, but not the loss of personal existence: on the contrary, in the stillness of mind there is an intense personal communion between a human person and a personal God.

The state of stillness of mind is related to 'wonder' and 'contemplation': it surpasses the boundary of pure prayer. According to Isaac,

... there is awestruck wonder and not prayer. For what pertains to prayer has ceased, while a certain divine vision (te'orya, contemplation) remains, and the mind does not pray a prayer. ... Prayer is one thing, and contemplation during prayer is another, even though each takes its inception from the other. For prayer is the seed, and the contemplation is the harvesting of the sheaves. Whence the reaper stands in ecstasy before the unutterable sight, how from the mean and naked seed which he sowed, such rich ears of wheat have suddenly burst forth before his eyes; then he remains entirely motionless in his contemplation.

In Isaac's teaching on stillness of mind, the influence of Evagrius Ponticus is unmistakable. When speaking of the state of stillness characterized by the 'inebriation' of the mind under the influence of the Holy Spirit, Isaac directly quotes Evagrius:

For the Holy Spirit moves in each man according to his measure,... so that ... his prayer is bereaved of movement, and his influence is confounded and swallowed up in awestruck wonder. ... The intellect's movements are immersed in a profound inebriation, and it is not in this world; at such a time there will be no distinction between soul and body, nor the remembrance of anything, even as the great and divine Evagrius said: 'Prayer is the settled state of the intellect, and it is terminated only by the light of the Holy Trinity through awestruck wonder'. ... And again the same Evagrius writes: 'Purity of the intellect is the lofty flight of the noetic faculties, which resembles the hue of the sky, and upon and through which the light of the Holy Trinity shines at the time of prayer'.

Isaac goes on to develop the evagrian notion of the intellect's vision of its own luminous nature, as well as the teaching of Dionysius the Areopagite on the 'blessed unknowing' that surpasses all human knowledge:

When the intellect puts off the old man and puts on the new man of grace, then it sees its purity to be like unto heaven's hue, which was also called the 'place of God' by the council of elders of Israel, when it was seen by them in the mountain. Therefore, as I have said, one must not call this grace and gift spiritual prayer, but the offspring of pure prayer which is engulfed by the Holy Spirit. At that moment the intellect is yonder, above prayer, and by the discovery of something better, prayer is abandoned. Then the intellect does not pray with prayer, but it gazes in ecstasy on incomprehensible things which surpass this mortal world, and it is silenced by its ignorance of all that is found there. This is the unknowing which has been called more sublime than knowledge.

Spiritual prayer, according to Isaac, is participation in the age to come, an experience of paradise on earth. The experience of contemplation which the saints enjoy in the future life is given to some during their earthly life through 'spiritual prayer':

The soul does not pray a prayer, but in awareness she perceives the spiritual things of that other age which transcend human conception; and the understanding of these is but the power of the Holy Spirit. This is noetic contemplation, not the movement and entreaty of prayer, although it has its starting-point in prayer.

In Isaac's teaching on spiritual prayer and stillness of mind are outlined all of the major themes of his mystical theology—themes such as contemplation, spiritual vision, wonder, 'inebriation', unknowing. Each of them will be discussed below.

2. CONTEMPLATION

Among the mystical terms found in Isaac's writings, the term te'orya (from the Greek theoria), draws our attention. Isaac borrowed this term from the language of Evagrius and Dionysius the Areopagite. In early syriac writers, including Aphrahat, Ephrem, Narsai, and Jacob of Sarug, the term does not occur. John the Solitary was probably the first syriac writer to use this term; in the sixth and seventh centuries the term is used by those east-syrian writers who were acquainted with the writings of Evagrius. In the context of mystical theology the term is normally translated as 'contemplation'. Isaac translates it into Syriac as 'spiritual vision'.

The term 'contemplation' occurs in Isaac in conjunction with a number of adjectives: essential, divine, hidden, exact, noetic, single, natural, angelic, exalted, spiritual, lofty, true, heavenly, and still others. Isaac talks about the contemplation of mysteries, of the Being of the Divinity, of divine care, of the creative activity of God, of created things, of the properties of Christ, of wisdom, of noetic things, of the Scriptures, of the angels, of prayer, of truth, of light, of glory. As Sebastian Brock has shown, many of these phrases he borrowed from the language of Evagrius, but some appear to be innovations by Isaac himself. Being primarily interested here in theoria as a mystical phenomenon, we shall limit ourselves to looking at certain texts on the contemplation of God and of the reality of the immaterial world.

In Isaac the term 'contemplation' very often appears as a synonym for 'vision of God'. He speaks of the supernatural state of the soul, 'her movement in the contemplation of the transubstantial Deity'. In this state, the soul rushes forward ... and on the wings of faith she soars aloft, taking leave of visible creation; she becomes as one drunken in awestruck wonder of her continual solicitude for God; and by simple, uncompounded vision, and by unseeing intuitions concerning the Divine Nature.

At the same time Isaac emphasizes that the righteous cannot see the essence of God. When someone is raised to the contemplation of God, one sees not God's essence, but 'the dark cloud of his glory'. One can see only a reflection of God's essence, though this vision will be fuller in the age to come:

The more a man becomes perfect with respect to God, the more he follows after him. But in the age of truth, God will show him His face, although not His essence. For however much the righteous enter into the contemplation of Him, they behold an enigma of His vision, like an image that is seen through a mirror; but yonder they behold the revelation of the truth.

Isaac speaks of contemplation-theoria as a high mystical state which very few people have attained:

It is not possible that even one in a thousand righteous men should be accounted worthy of this lofty noetic perception. And indeed, the theoria concerning our Lord's incarnation and his manifestation in the flesh is also said to arise from theoria concerning the Divinity.

Besides the contemplation of God in his nature and his actions, contemplation of the angelic powers 'in their very nature and their own realm' is also possible. This angelic contemplation is to be distinguished from visions in which angels appear to people in visible forms. Such visions are not a true vision, but only a manifestation to encourage the simple. Only the contemplation of the angels in their own invisible realm is true contemplation: it 'belongs to illumined and wise men who have been exalted by the glorious discipline of stillness to the rank of purity'.

Isaac also draws a distinction between 'natural (kyanayta) contemplation'—that is, the one related to the nature of the soul—and 'spiritual (ruhanayta) contemplation', which is a supernatural gift of God. The first is characteristic of human beings in their primordial natural state before the fall; the second is reserved to the blessed life of the age to come:

This contemplation brings the soul close to the nakedness of the intellect which is called immaterial theoria. And this is the spiritual discipline. For it lifts up the understanding from earthly things, brings it close to the spirit's pristine theoria, and presents it to God through the divine vision of that unutterable pristine glory. ... This is the discipline written about by the Fathers, namely that whenever the intellects of the saints receive hypostatic theoria, then even the body's grossness is taken away, and from thenceforward their vision becomes spiritual. Now 'hypostatic theoria' refers to the created state of man's primordial nature. And from this hypostatic vision a man is easily moved and led up to what is called unitary knowledge, which is, in plain terms, awestruck wonder at God. This is the state of the majestical way of life to come, which is granted in the freedom of immortal life in existence after the resurrection.

Contemplation of God becomes in Isaac an experience of the departure from this world and participation in the world to come. This eschatological character of the contemplation of God is stressed by Isaac's claim that the kingdom of heaven is 'spiritual contemplation' (te'orya ruhanayta). The experience of this kingdom begins in earthly life and continues in the age to come. Yet in this life only very few are counted worthy of this gift, mostly ascetics and solitaries who renounce the world:

A spiritual theoria ... is arrayed in luminous intuitions. He who possesses it will not gaze searchingly at the world again nor will he cleave to his body. ... If God would send forth this true theoria to mankind but for a short while, the world would remain without succeeding generations. This divine vision is a bond before which nature cannot stand, and it proves to be for the man who has received this meditation in his soul a God-given grace. ... It is given especially to those concerning whom God knows that they must truly withdraw from the world to a better life because of the good volition that he has found in them. But it increases and abides with them when they dwell in a secluded and solitary place. Let us make entreaty for this contemplation in our prayers. Let us keep long vigils for the sake of it. And let us beseech the Lord with tears that he grant us this as a gift which has no equal.

The contemplation of God, Isaac asserts, occurs in the presence of angels:

When by the in-working of divine grace there suddenly arise within us great thoughts and astonishment at the intellect's contemplations, which are more lofty than nature, and when, as Saint Evagrius says, the holy angels draw nigh to us, filling us with spiritual vision, then all things that oppose us retreat and there is peace and ineffable tranquillity for as long a time as we remain in these things.

When Isaac speaks of 'angelic contemplation' (te'orya mal'akayta), and of 'heavenly contemplations' (te'oryas šmayyanyata) in which the intellect is 'moved without the senses by the spiritual powers of those worlds on high which possess wonders without number', his phraseology is meant to point to the presence of the angelic world when one contemplates divine realities.

In his teaching on contemplation-theoria, Isaac was under the influence of the hierarchical system of Dionysius the Areopagite, according to which contemplation of God is impossible for human beings except through the mediation of the angels. Divine revelations are transmitted from God to the angels through the mediation of Jesus, and then from the angels to human beings. Echoing the Areopagite, Isaac says of the hierarchical order of transmission of divine revelation from God to human beings:

The angels are our teachers, even as they are for one another; for the lower ones are taught by those who oversee them and possess more light, and so each order is illuminated from the one above even up to that one order that possesses the Holy Trinity as teacher. And further, this very first order says openly that it is not instructed of itself, but it has as its teacher Jesus the Mediator, from whom it receives and then transmits to those below it. It is my opinion that our intellect does not have a natural power to be moved to the contemplation of Divinity. … Although we, human beings, should purify and cleanse ourselves, yet without the mediation of angels our intellect will not be able to attain to the revelations and insights which lead to that essential divine vision which is the true revelation of mysteries. For our intellect does not have a capacity as great as that of the most sublime beings, who without mediation receive revelations and divine visions from the Eternal One.

In the age to come, the saints will contemplate God face to face, while in this present life contemplation is possible only through the mediation of angels:

Whenever the perception of the revelation of a mystery descends into the intellects of the saints, this is also from the angels. When it is permitted by God, a mystery is revealed from a higher angelic order to a lower one, even unto the lowest; and in the same manner, when it is permitted by the divine nod that a mystery should come even to human nature, it is transmitted by those who are wholly worthy of it. For by their intermediary the saints receive the light of divine vision, leading even to the glorious Eternal Being, the mystery which cannot be taught. … In the future age, however, this order of things will be abolished. For then one will not receive from another the revelation of God's glory unto the gladness and joy of his soul; but to each by himself the Master will give according to the measure of his excellence and his worthiness.

3. VISIONS, REVELATIONS, INSIGHTS

'Vision' (ḥzata) and 'revelation' (gelyana) are terms closely associated with 'contemplation'. Whereas contemplation depends on the mediation of angels, visions and revelations are often an immediate contact with the world on high. At the same time, as we shall see, angels can take part in visions, but their function in them is not limited to mediation between God and a human person; rather, in visions they act in an independent role as messengers of divine mysteries.

Isaac defines the 'divine vision' (ḥzata alahaya) as a 'non-sensible revelation to the intellect'. 'Vision' and 'revelation' are often regarded by Isaac as synonyms. There is, however, a certain semantic difference between them, which is indicated in the following passage:

Question: Are vision and revelation the same, or different?

Answer: No, they are different. Revelation is often said with respect to the two, because what is hidden is revealed and something once hidden now becomes manifest by some means. Not every revelation is a vision, but every vision is called a revelation, because what is hidden is revealed. Still, not all becomes revealed and known through a vision. Revelation is received for the most part concerning things that are known, tasted and perceived by the intellect. But vision comes to pass in many ways, as it were in likeness and in types, even as it was given in olden times to the ancients, whether in deep sleep or waking. Sometimes it was precise, sometimes as though in an apparition and somehow obscurely. For often the very man who beholds the vision does not know whether the thing had truly taken place or it occurred as though in a dream. It also happens that a voice of succour is heard, at times a certain form is seen, at times a more distinct vision, that is, face to face, and sight, and speech, and questions and the ensuing intercourse. These things occur in desert wildernesses and places far removed from men, where a man is by necessity in great need of them because he has no help or comfort from any quarter. But the revelations that are perceived by the intellect through its purity are received by perfect men alone who are replete with knowledge.

Revelation is therefore higher than vision. Revelation, moreover, is a more general concept than vision. The term 'revelation' refers to the inward mystical experience; 'vision' indicates concrete and visible appearances from the immaterial world. To the realm of visions belong in particular, the appearances of angels to saints and martyrs:

Let the holy martyrs be examples to encourage you. The martyrs, often many together but sometimes one alone, in places both many and diverse, contested for Christ's sake. … To such as these, the holy angels would manifestly appear. … But what need is there to speak of the ascetics, those strangers to the world, and of the anchorites, who made the desert a city and a dwelling-place and hostelry of angels? For the angels would continually visit these men because their modes of life were so similar. … And since, having abandoned things earthly, they loved the heavenly and were become imitators of the angels, rightly did those very same holy angels not conceal the sight of themselves from them… .

Not only angels, but also departed saints appear to ascetics in dream:

Those who are near to attaining the stage of purity are deemed worthy always to behold certain of the saints during the vision of the night; and at every moment during the day, the vision of them, which has been engraved upon their souls, produces in these men the food of joy through their intellect's noetic rumination.

'Revelation' refers to the inner contiguity of a person with an unearthly reality; it does not necessarily presuppose seeing a certain visible image. Most frequently the term is used in the plural:

The beginning of spiritual contemplation … is the beginning of every revelation in the intellect; by this activity the intellect grows and becomes powerful in hidden things, and by this the intellect advances to other revelations which surpass the nature of man. In a word,… all divine contemplation and all revelations of the Spirit which the saints receive in this world, and whatever gifts and revelations human nature can come to know in this life, pass over to a man.

Here revelations are spoken of as a phenomenon which accompanies the intellect in different stages of its development: the way of the intellect is regarded as a way from one revelation to another.

'Revelations', in Isaac's vocabulary, are the experience of participation in the kingdom of heaven during one's earthly life:

The revelation of the good that is hidden within us is the apperception of knowledge of truth: 'The Kingdom of heaven is mystically within you'… Wonder at the divine nature is a revelation of the New World. Revelations of the New World are wondrous stirrings concerning God. With these mysteries all rational nature will be stirred in that future existence, in that heavenly abode. The holy powers exist now by means of these impulses: this is the mode of life of angels, so that they are astonished at this mystery all the time, due to revelations that come upon them in various ways during these stirrings concerning the Divine Nature. This is the exalted position which life after the resurrection holds.

Isaac distinguishes between the revelations 'of the New World' and the revelations 'about the New World'. The first are meetings with the divine reality; the second are spiritual insights into the eschatological 'future state' of the created world:

The revelations of the New World are quite different from the revelations about the New World. The former concern the glorious nature of the divine Majesty; the latter concern the wondrous transformations which creation will experience, and concern each aspect of the future state as it is made known to the intellect through the revelation of various insights, which in turn are the result of continual reflection on them and illumination.

In one of the chapters in Part I, Isaac speaks of the six kinds of revelations which are mentioned in Scripture: through the senses; by means of physical sight; through the rapture of the spirit; 'by the rank of prophecy'; 'in some intellectual way'; and 'as if by dream'. Revelations through the senses are either 'those which take place by means of the elements'—the Burning Bush, for example, or the cloud of God's glory—or those 'without matter' and yet experienced 'by means of the bodily senses'—like the appearance of the three men to Abraham or Jacob's ladder. Revelation through physical sight occurred, for example, when Isaiah saw the Lord sitting on a high throne with seraphs around him. 'Rapture in spirit' is what happened to Paul when he was taken up to the third heaven, yet whether this was in or out of the body, he did not know. Revelation 'by the rank of prophesy' refers to 'the things that happened unto the Prophets, who foretold future events many ages before they took place'. Revelation 'in some intellectual way' gives a certain insight into the Divine Nature or the resurrection of the dead or the age to come or some other key dogma of the christian faith. Finally, the revelation 'by dream' is one given to someone during his sleep.

Isaac claims that revelations take place both 'by means of images' and 'without images'. Those with images are given by God to instruct many people and give them 'a small insight' into truth. Those 'without images' are usually given to a single person, to instruct, comfort, and console him. However, Isaac emphasizes, such revelations should not be taken as equal to the whole truth and perfect knowledge, as they are only insights into this truth and reveal it according to the strength of the human nature.

The term 'insights' (sukkale) is therefore semantically close to the term 'revelations': it, too, is used in the plural and can serve as a description of sudden and bright contiguity with the reality of the other world. Insights differ from revelations by their more swift, impetuous character; they are instantaneous, but leave a deep trace on a person's soul. Insights can take place at various stages of a Christian's spiritual life:

There is the person who has reached perfection on the level of the soul, but who has not yet entered the mode of life of the spirit: only a little of it has begun to stir in him. While he is fully in the mode of life of the soul, every now and then it happens that some stirrings of the spirit arise indistinctly in him, and he begins to perceive in his soul a hidden joy and consolation: like flashes of lightning … particular mystical insights arise and are set in motion in his mind. At this his heart at once bursts with joy. … I know a person living in the vicinity who experiences these lightning flashes. But even though insight into mysteries momentarily passes through his mind and then departs, nevertheless the outburst of joy at the experience lasts a long time, and then after it goes, serenity resulting from it is poured over the mind for a considerable period. Furthermore, the condition of the body and the limbs becomes one of peace, and they feel great rest, while the enjoyment of the sweetness of its wondrous character is marked at the supreme moment on the mind's palate.

'Insights' are such spiritual boosts which suddenly arise in a person during prayer or reading. A person's intellect then enters into the Holy of Holies and communicates with God. At that moment, as in the case with 'stillness of mind', prayer ceases:

The word 'prayer'… refers to a period of standing or a particular act of worship; for while engaged in his reading, an ascetic is never for one moment devoid of the upsurges of prayer. For no reading of Scripture which has engaged in this spiritual concern will be empty of the fountain of prayer, seeing that for the most part this person will be inebriated by the mysteries he encounters. Profound prayers will appear unawares in him in a wondrous way, without his having prepared or willed them. And why do I call 'prayer' his frequently being inebriated by some insight, seeing that no place is to be found there any longer for the stirring or recollection of prayer? This is something much more excellent—insofar as this can be said—even than the level of prayer. Prayer, however, is lower in rank than being stirred in spirit: on this there is no dispute, for prayer is inferior to this mystery. Frequently, when the intellect is stirred by some insight produced by events either in the natural world or in the Scriptures as it perceives their spiritual intention and then peers, with the help of the grace which accompanies it, into the Holy of Holies of their mysteries, then there is not even the strength to pray. … When the intellect is given permission and accorded the strength to enter therein, no strength or movement or activity is left remaining in the senses during these periods. There is someone from among those who are gathered here who has always experienced these things: I know that his heart immediately leaps up when he encounters this kind of reading which comes from the experience and from indications of the things just mentioned.

Visions, revelations, and insights can therefore be spoken of as different aspects of the same phenomenon: a human person's encounter with the realities of the immaterial world. 'Visions' refers to encounters with personal beings (angels, saints) who dwell in that world and who appear in visible form; 'revelations' denotes spiritual penetration into the Divine Being or the eschatological, renewed created world; 'insights' signifies mystical flashes within a person's intellect, when suddenly, during prayer or reading, the mysteries of the other world are opened to him.

4. 'OVERSHADOWING' AND 'ILLUMINATION'

Two other mystical terms in Isaac the Syrian point to an action of divine grace upon a human person. They are 'overshadowing' and 'illumination'. Connected with illumination is Isaac's mysticism of light, which we will also consider here.

The term maggnanuta, which can be translated as 'overshadowing' or 'tabernacling', refers to a specific action by a higher power upon a lower. In Isaac, 'overshadowing' refers to the influence of the Holy Spirit over a person. Isaac begins by defining the term and indicating its use in the Bible:

'Overshadowing' is a term indicating help and protection, and also the receiving of a heavenly gift; for example, 'The Holy Spirit shall come and the power of the Most High shall overshadow you'. The former kind is involved in 'Cause your right hand, Lord, to overshadow me', which is a request for help; this is like 'I will overshadow this town and deliver it'. Thus we understand two kinds of action in the 'overshadowing' over human beings that comes from God: one is mysterious [sacramental] and spiritual [noetic], the other practical.

The first kind of overshadowing, continues Isaac,

consists in the sanctification which is received through divine grace; in other words, when, through the operation of the Holy Spirit, someone is sanctified in his body and soul, as was the case with Elisabeth, John the Baptist, and the holy Mary, blessed among women—although in her case it was unique, going beyond the case of other created being.

A similar overshadowing happens to every saint who is deemed worthy of divine revelation and the action of the Holy Spirit:

The mysterious variety of overshadowing such as takes place with any holy person is an active force which overshadows the intellect, and when someone is held worthy of this overshadowing, the intellect is seized and dilated with a sense of wonder, in a kind of divine revelation. As long as this divine activity overshadows the intellect, the person is raised above the movement of the thoughts of his soul, thanks to the participation of the Holy Spirit. ... This is one mysterious kind of overshadowing: when this power overshadows a person, he is held worthy of the glory of the New World by means of revelation. This is the partial overshadowing which has been the lot of the 'saints in light', as the blessed Paul said, of which those are held worthy who have received from the Spirit sanctification of the intellect through their holy and excellent way of life.

In the second kind of overshadowing, divine activity becomes known to a person by experience, and it is

a spiritual power which protects and hovers over someone continuously, driving from him anything harmful which may happen to approach his body and soul. This is something which is perceived invisibly by the illumined intellect that has knowledge by means of the eye of faith... .

Both the first and the second overshadowings have then a mystical character. The second is accompanied by the 'invisible vision'—that is, the experience of contemplating the invisible reality which is accessible to the 'illumined intellect'—and the term is therefore semantically akin to 'vision' and 'contemplation'.

The term nahhiruta, 'illumination', also refers to the influence of divine grace over a person. Derived from nuhra, 'light', it points to an action of God within a person which is accompanied by the presence of light. Isaac develops the theme of illumination in Chapter VI of Part II:

I will give you two genuine signs, my brother, and at the time when God holds you worthy to be illumined inwardly, you will, thanks to them, be aware of the light of your soul. They are the following, and are sufficient to indicate the truth which has begun to shine out in your soul. When, through the grace and mercy of our Lord Jesus Christ, that illumination of mind of which the Fathers speak has begun to shine in you, there are two signs which will give you confirmation of this. ... Now one of the signs is this: once this hidden light starts shining in your soul you will have the sign, that whenever you leave off the reading Scripture or prayer, the mind will be caught up with certain verses or with the content of these, and it will meditate on, examine and probe of its own accord into their spiritual significance; it will be so bound up with them that it will not depart from them and be distracted by anything else in creation. ... The second sign, which is as precise as the first, is the following: when the soul leaves the darkness and becomes light from within, then prolonged kneelings are granted to the solitary, and tarrying in them will prove so delightful that he may be three days kneeling on the ground in prayer, without his knowing any fatigue as a result of the delight,... and the delightfulness of prayer has become so strong in him, that his tongue stands still and his heart becomes silent. In this way a delightful stillness takes hold of his heart and his limbs to such an extent that he does not even conceive, one might say, of the kingdom of heaven as being comparable in its delightfulness to this stillness in prayer. ... Accordingly, in measure with the manner and extent to which someone enters illumination of mind, so will he be held worthy of delight in kneeling.

In speaking here of an illumination that occurs in a rather leisurely and invisible manner and is recognized by external signs rather than by internal feeling, Isaac clearly points to the nature of the light of which he speaks: it is 'the light of the soul', or 'the soul which becomes light'. The soul exits from darkness and begins to see its own natural light.

The term 'light' (nuhra) is frequently encountered in Isaac's writings, but it usually refers not to a visible and concrete light, nor is it the divine light seen by mystics. If Isaac knew the experience of the vision of the divine light spoken of by syriac and byzantine mystical writers—John of Dalyatha, Symeon the New Theologian, Gregory Palamas, and many others—he never described it in detail. Isaac cannot in this sense be considered a predecessor of byzantine hesychasm. Readers accustomed to the greek text of Isaac or translations from it will immediately remember phrases like 'the light of the Holy Trinity', which shines, like the sun, in a person's soul, and 'contemplation of the Holy Trinity'. None of them, however, occurs in authentic writings of Isaac, but are found either in works of John of Dalyatha and Philoxenus of Mabbug attributed to him, or in Isaac's quotations from Evagrius.

In authentic texts, the phrase 'divine light' (nuhra alahaya) does not carry the specific and concrete character which it receives in hesychast literature. The same is true of the phrases 'the light of theoria', 'the holy light', and the like. All these expressions refer to an inward experience of spiritual vision, that is, the ascetic's vision of the light of his own soul as a result of illumination from above which has taken place in his intellect. This is the content of the passage on illumination quoted above. The notion of the natural light of the human soul was known to Evagrius: he speaks of the 'inner man' who has become a 'gnostic' contemplating 'the light of the beauty of his soul' (nuhra d-šupra d-napšeh). Evagrius distinguished between the divine light—which is the light of the Holy Trinity—and the natural light of the human soul which is contemplated by ascetics during prayer. Isaac does quote Evagrius' texts concerning the vision of the light of the Holy Trinity, but in his own writings he speaks more regularly of the inner and hidden light of the human soul.

The sources of spiritual illumination and of the radiance of the light within the soul are prayer and ascetical activities. Reflection 'on the ministry of righteousness' is also a source of spiritual illumination, as are the memory of God and night vigil:

Good soil which gladdens its husbandman by bringing forth fruit an hundredfold is a soul that is made radiant by the remembrance of God and unsleeping vigil both day and night. The Lord establishes on her steadfastness a cloud that overshadows her by day and with a flaming light he illumines her by night: within her darkness a light shines.

Kneelings with contrition may also contribute to inner illumination:

At whatever time God may open up your thinking from within, give yourself over to unremitting bows and prostrations. ... Then light will dawn within you, and your righteousness will quickly shine forth, and you will be like a paradise of burgeoning flowers and an unfailing fountain of waters.

The radiance of the light in one's own soul is a source of constant spiritual joy:

Until someone loses the faith which is in his heart—by this I mean the certain knowledge of this divine care which will prevent him from falling into darkness of mind, from which comes anxiety and anguish—for otherwise his soul is filled all the time with light and joy, and it exults continually—that person dwells as though in heaven in the illumination of his thoughts which the faith of his heart instills in him; and from this point on he is also held worthy of the revelation of insights.

The theme of spiritual joy brings us to a discussion of mystical 'wonder', another important feature of Isaac's mysticism.

5. WONDER

One of the most characteristic spiritual states to be described by mystical writers is ecstasy, commonly accompanied by a feeling of spiritual elevation and compunction, tears and, not infrequently, loss of self-consciousness, weakening of the bodily members, and withdrawal of the mind from the body. The greek word ekstasis—which literally means 'separation' or 'withdrawal'—does not have a direct counterpart in Syriac: the closest equivalents are the terms temha and tehra, both of which are translated as 'wonder', 'astonishment', or 'amazement'. Temha is more frequent in Isaac, who uses it to refer to the same mystical state that was called ekstasis by the greek mystical authors; in the greek version of Isaac both temha and tehra are normally translated as ekstasis.

The state of wonder is closely linked in Isaac to the states of the 'stillness of mind' and 'spiritual contemplation', described above. 'When someone receives all the time an awareness of these mysteries', Isaac writes, by means of that interior eye which is called spiritual contemplation (te'orya d-ruḥ), which consists in a mode of vision provided by grace, then the moment he becomes aware of one of these mysteries, his heart is at once rendered serene with a kind of wonder. Not only do the lips cease from the flow of prayer and become still, but the heart too dries up from all thoughts, because of the amazement that overcomes it; and it receives by grace the sweetness of the mysteries of God's wisdom and love by means of the mode of vision which has knowledge of events and natural beings.

Wonder may stem from various sources. It can be a fruit of withdrawal from the world and a solitary life: 'The soul's separation from the world and her stillness naturally move her towards the understanding of God's creatures. And by this she is lifted up toward God; being astonished, she is struck with wonder, and she remains with God'. Wonder/astonishment can be born of prayerful meditation: 'For stillness and … meditation … kindle great and endless sweetness in the heart and swiftly draw the intellect to unspeakable astonishment'. Wonder/ecstasy may come from the reading of Scripture. It can also emerge from the recollection of God: 'From long continuance in his recollection, a man is transported at times to astonishment and wonder'. Isaac points to the action of the Holy Spirit as a cause of wonder:

Just as with certain species of trees, sweetness comes upon them as a result of the sun, likewise, when the Spirit shines out in our hearts, then the movements of our meditation—which is called 'spiritual conduct'—are brought close to luminosity; then our intellect, not through any act of will on its part, is drawn up, by means of some kind of reflection, in wonder towards God.

We find several kinds of wonder in Isaac's writings. They differ from one another by the intensity of the ascetic's mystical experience. The first kind of wonder is a spiritual amazement which occurs during prayer or while reading Scripture. A person does not lose a self-control, though his mind may be entirely 'captured' by God:

… he forgets even himself and his nature. He becomes like a man in ecstasy, who has no recollection at all of this age. With special diligence he ponders and reflects upon what pertains to God's majesty. … And so the ascetic, being engrossed in these marvels and continually struck with wonder, is always drunken as he lives, as it were, in the life after the resurrection. … When he becomes intoxicated with these things, he is once again translated from thence hither by his divine vision concerning this age in which he still abides and he says, stricken with astonishment: 'O the depth of the riches of the wisdom, knowledge, insight, prudence and economy of the inscrutable God!'. … Then as one in ecstasy he muses and says: 'How long will this age continue? When will the future age commence? … How will that mode of life come to be? In what form will this nature be resurrected and framed? In what manner will it undergo a second creation?'. … Then he stands up, bends his knees, and with many tears offers up thanksgiving and glorification to the God who alone is wise …

The second kind of wonder is accompanied by a weakening of bodily members:

It often happens that when a man bends his knees in prayer and stretches his hands to the heavens, fixing his eyes upon the cross of Christ and concentrating all his thoughts on God during his prayer, beseeching God all the while with tears and compunction, suddenly and without warning a fountain springs up in his heart gushing forth sweetness: his members grow feeble, his eyesight is veiled, he bows his head to the earth, and his thoughts are altered so that because of the joy which surges throughout his entire body he cannot make prostrations.

The third kind of wonder is characterized by a loss of the sense of one's corporeality, loss of self-consciousness, and withdrawal of the mind from the body. Isaac speaks of the state of an ascetic when 'ecstasy, awestruck wonder and stillness overcome him and his perception of his corporeality is stolen away, and for a long time he abides in silence'. There are ancient saints known to have spent several hours or even days in this state:

For we see that when Saint Anthony was standing at the prayer of the ninth hour, he perceived that his intellect was taken up. And when another Father stretched out his hands while standing at prayer, he entered an ecstasy for the period of four days. And likewise many others through prayer were taken captive by their strong recollection of God and their love for him, and thus came to ecstasy.

Isaac tells us of a contemporary who told him: 'When I wish to get up for my office, I am permitted to say a single marmita; but as for the rest, if I stand for three days, I am in awestruck wonder with God, and feel no weariness at all'.

A special kind of wonder is described by Isaac in a homily in Part I which was included neither in the west-syrian recension nor in the greek translation. It is a wonder which begins in sleep, causes the sleeper to awake, and continues after he has risen. Isaac is probably describing his own experience here. He uses the third person singular, but this is a convention in such cases:

I myself know a man who even during sleep was seized with awestruck wonder at God through theoria on something from the material of his evening's reading. And while his soul was astonished at the meditation of this divine vision, he perceived as it were that for a long time he was dwelling upon the thoughts of his sleep and delving into the marvel of that vision. It was, indeed, in the very deep of night when suddenly he awoke from his sleep, his tears flowing like streams and falling even to his chest. His mouth was filled with glorifications and his heart mused long upon that divine vision with sweetness that knew no satiety. From the abundance of his tears, which without measure spilled from his pupils, and from the stupefaction of his soul, whereby all the members of his body became limp, and of his heart, wherein a certain sweetness throbbed, he was not even able to perform his usual liturgy of night prayer. Only with difficulty could he utter a psalm at daybreak, so overwhelmed was he by the multitude of his tears which gushed involuntarily from the fountains of his eyes... .

Isaac often speaks of the joy which rises up in a person in a state of wonder. It is a supernatural and divine joy that comes from a feeling of freedom and love of God, and it is accompanied by a liberation from fear:

So once a person has been raised up above the ministry on the level of the soul in his reflection and understanding ... and is being raised up to the mode of the life of the spirit,... immediately a state of wonder at God (tehra dbalaha) attaches itself to him, and he becomes serene and tranquil after the stirrings of his former thoughts, as his entire mind vibrates with spiritual stirrings, accompanied by love. In this state of understanding, fear is removed from a person, and after the manner of that New World, the mind is stirred with freedom from thoughts concerning any fear or suffering incurred in reflection. ... He is in a state of joy of soul, and in his reflection and thoughts he is quite unlike those who belong to this world, for he exists henceforth in freedom from thoughts, a freedom which is filled with stirrings of knowledge and wonder at God. And because he exists in a state of understanding which is more lofty than the soul, and exalted above fear, he is in a state of joy at God in the stirring of his thoughts at all the times—as befits the rank of children.

Joy and wonder at God can become an abiding experience. Even so, as Isaac emphasizes, joy in mystical experience is intermingled with suffering. The joy derives from a sense of the fervent love of God and the unspeakable closeness of God to the person; the suffering, from the impossibility of remaining in this state uninterruptedly. In this sense, Isaac claims, 'there is no suffering more burning than the love of God'. And immediately adds: 'O Lord, hold me worthy to taste of this fountain!' The closer a person is to God, the more his thirst for communion with God increases, and it is thirst that cannot be slaked. This is why joy and suffering are lived through simultaneously; they are two different aspects of one and the same experience:

... through that sweet suffering that takes place in the mind for the sake of God at the life-resorting sorrow of which the Apostle spoke the following are born in the mind in accordance with the various directions its meditating takes: grief for the sake of God or joy at him; and a heart that is dilated with the hope for which it continually peers out. With their sharp warmth this suffering and joy burn and scorch the body, drying it up at the seething infusion of blood which provides heat and spreads through the veins; for the flame of the mind's stirrings as a result of the fervour of the hidden ministry heats up the body's constitution. This hidden ministry causes a wondrous sort of transformation to erupt all the time, which either gives joy to both soul and body or anguishes it with a sharp suffering.

The state of wonder which ascetics experience during their lifetime is a symbol of that wonder in which the saints live in the age to come; it is 'a taste of the kingdom of heaven' and 'a revelation of the New World'. To support his teaching, Isaac draws on Evagrius:

And this is what Evagrius, recipient of boundless spiritual revelations, names 'the hundred-fold reward which our Lord promised in his Gospel'. In his wonder at the greatness of this delight he did well to call it 'the key to the kingdom of heaven'. I say in truth, as before God, that the body's limbs are incapable of holding up before this delight, and the heart is incapable of receiving it because of the magnitude of its pleasure. What more is there to say, seeing that the saints name it 'the apperception of the kingdom of heaven'. For it is a symbol of that future wonder at God,... when the intellect is raised up, as though on a ladder, to him who is the kingdom of the saints, and it abides in wonder. Well has this apperception been called 'the mystery of the kingdom of heaven', for we are, during these mysteries, in a state of knowledge of him who is the true kingdom of all.

6. 'INEBRIATION' WITH THE LOVE OF GOD

To the term 'wonder', 'inebriation' (rawwayuta) is semantically close and it is used by Isaac to describe an especially strong experience of the love of God, and the joy and spiritual elevation of a state of mystical ecstasy. 'Sober inebriation' is a central theme in the christian mystical tradition from Origen and Gregory of Nyssa onwards. In the syriac tradition, this theme is outlined as early as Ephrem and John of Apamea, and it was developed by Dadisho and Symeon d–Taibutheh. For Isaac the Syrian, the theme of spiritual inebriation constitutes a synthesis of the whole system of his mystical theology: by analyzing it, we can perceive the most characteristic traits of his mysticism.

In one of the chapters of Part II, while speaking of the state of wonder which begins beyond the borders of prayer, Isaac uses the image of wine to describe the spiritual exaltation which grips a person:

Sometimes … while prayer remains for its part, the intellect is taken away from it as if into heaven, and tears fall like fountains of waters, involuntarily soaking the whole face. All this time such a person is serene, still and filled with a wonder-filled vision. Very often he will not be allowed even to pray: this in truth is the state of cessation above prayer when he remains continually in amazement at God's work of creation—like people who are crazed by wine, for this is 'the wine which causes the person's heart to rejoice'… . Blessed is the person who has entered this door in the experience of his own soul, for all the power of ink, letters and phrases is too feeble to indicate the delight of this mystery.

Isaac most frequently uses the symbol of inebriation in speaking of how the love of God seizes someone's soul. According to Isaac, love is a gift which cannot be acquired by human effort. Ascetical activity, including the reading of Scripture, is conducive to the attaining of love, but love cannot appear in a person unless it is given from above. To taste love by reading books is impossible: one can only eat or drink it oneself. 'Love of God', Isaac writes,… cannot be stirred up in someone solely as a result of knowledge of the Scriptures; nor can anyone love God by forcing himself. What is possible is for the mind to receive, from the reading and recounting of Scripture and knowledge of it, a sense of reverence which stems from a recollection of the majesty of God. … Not even as a result of the law, or commandment which He gives concerning love, is it possible to love God: from the law there comes a sense of awe, but not one of desire. For until a person receives the Spirit of revelation and his soul, with its impulses, is united to that wisdom which is above the world and he becomes aware in his own person of God's lofty attributes, it is not possible for him to come close to this glorious savour of love. Someone who has not actually drunk (ešti) wine will not be inebriated as a result of being told about wine; and someone who has not been himself held worthy (eštwi) of a knowledge of the lofty things of God cannot become inebriated with love for him.

The symbolism of wine and inebriation opens to Isaac the possibility of describing phenomena of the mystical life which are otherwise difficult to express in words. The thirst for God which is characteristic of periods of abandonment, for example, is symbolized by the alcoholic thirst of a drinker deprived of wine:

With a laudable ecstasy the heart soars up toward God and cries out: 'My soul thirsted for thee, the mighty, the living God! When shall I come and appear before Thy face,

O Lord?' Only the man who drinks deeply of this wine and afterward is deprived of it, only he knows to what misery he has been abandoned, and what has been taken away from him because of his laxity.

Isaac likens the weakening of the limbs characteristic of certain kinds of ecstasy to the similar weakness in a state of intoxication:

Through such zealous and divine diligence … a man begins to be stirred to divine love and straightway he is made drunk by it as by wine; his limbs become limp, his mind stands still in awestruck wonder, and his heart follows God as a captive. He becomes, as I said, like a man drunk with wine.

The obliviousness to the cares and sorrows of this world brought on by inebriation with the love of God is compared with the forgetfulness of sorrows brought on by a state of intoxication by wine:

As a man who drinks wine and becomes inebriated on a day of mourning forgets all the pangs of his sorrow, so the man who in this world—which is a house of lamentation—is drunk with the love of God, forgets all his sorrows and afflictions and becomes insensible of all sinful passions through his inebriation'.

In the mystical life, a person's spiritual state changes as he becomes capable of experiences which were previously inaccessible to him. Instead of a contrite sorrow, a person lives through joy in God and to him another vision of the world opens, another perception of reality. This change of spiritual state is symbolized by a distorted apperception of reality characteristic of drunkenness:

Rightly directed labours and humility make man a god upon earth. Faith and mercy speed him on the way to limpid purity. Fervency and contrition of heart cannot dwell simultaneously in one soul, even as drunken men cannot have control of their thinking. For when the soul is given this fervour, the contrition of mourning is taken away. Wine has been given for gladness, and fervour for the rejoicing of the soul. The former warms the body, and the word of God, the understanding. Those who are inflamed by fervour are ravished by hope's meditations and their mind is caught away to the future age. Just as men drunken with wine imagine diverse hallucinations, even so men drunken and made fervent by hope are conscious neither of afflictions nor of anything worldly.

When speaking of that unearthly sweetness and delight characteristic of mystical experience, when even the body rejoices with the soul, Isaac emphasizes that these feelings cannot be described in words:

Does there blaze up within you a sudden joy that completely stills the tongue? Does a certain sweetness, which by reason of its delightfulness is beyond comparison, constantly well up from your heart and does it draw the whole man altogether after it? And at times does there imperceptibly descend into the whole body a certain delight and gladness—things which a tongue cannot express …? But whenever the delight which surges through his whole body sojourns within a man, at that hour he thinks that nothing save this is the kingdom of the heavens.

Again, the language of inebriation comes to Isaac's aid, helping him to describe the indescribable:

When the soul is drunk with the joy of hope and with the gladness which is in God, the body, even if it be feeble, becomes insensible to tribulations. ... And it enjoys and works together with the soul in her spiritual delight. So it is when the soul enters into spiritual joy even though the body may be weak.

The feeling of spiritual lightness during mystical experience, as well as the contact with the divine fire which penetrates the whole of a human person, is also described by analogy with intoxication:

Question: Why is hope so sweet, her discipline and her labors so light, and her works so easy for the soul?

Answer: Because hope awakens a natural longing in the soul and gives men this cup to drink, straightway making them drunk. Thenceforth they no longer feel the wearisome toil, but become insensitive to afflictions, and throughout the whole course of their journey they think that they are walking on air, and not treading the path with human footsteps. ... For this hope so inflames them, as with fire, that on account of their joy they cannot rest from their incessant and headlong course. There comes to pass in them what was spoken by the blessed Jeremiah, 'I said, I shall not remember Him nor speak His name. And there was in my heart as it were a flaming fire and it entered into my bones'. Such is the recollection of God in the hearts of men who are drunk with hope on his promises.

To the theme of inebriation, that of 'divine madness' or 'divine foolishness' is closely connected. This theme, also characteristic of many mystics, appeared as early as the epistles of Saint Paul, who opposed the 'foolishness' of the christian message to the 'wisdom' of this world, and the 'foolishness' of the christian way of life to worldly honour. Mystical writers frequently speak of madness and foolishness when they want to emphasize the paradoxical, unutterable, and super-rational character of an experience of communion with God. So it is that Isaac compares the inebriation and intoxication with God's love which accompanies a state of wonder with foolishness:

Love is fervent by nature, and when it descends beyond measure upon a man, it flings his soul into ecstasy. Therefore the heart of the person who has felt this love cannot contain it or endure it. ... This is the spiritual passion with which the apostles and the martyrs were inebriated. With it the first traveled the world over, toiling and being reviled, while the second, although their members were severed and although they shed their blood like water and suffered the most dreadful torments, yet they did not grow faint-hearted but endured courageously, and being truly wise, were thought fools. Still others wandered in mountains and caves and dens of the earth, and amid disorder they were well ordered. ... May God grant us also to attain to such madness!

Isaac speaks of mystical 'foolishness' as his own experience. Foolishness and madness is that love of God and neighbour which knows no bounds whatever and goes far beyond reasonable limits. The love one tastes is compared with honey which, like wine, symbolizes sweetness:

Someone who has attained to the love of God no longer wishes to remain in this life, for love abolishes fear. My beloved, I have become foolish, and I cannot bear to guard the mystery in silence, but I am become a fool for the sake of my brothers' profit. For true love is not able to tarry in any mystery without her beloved. Often when I was writing these things my fingers failed me in setting down everything on paper and they were unable to endure the sweetness that descended into my heart and silenced my senses. … Joy that is in God is stronger than this present life. … Love is sweeter than life, and understanding according to God,—from which love is begotten—is sweeter than honey in a honeycomb. What is this sweetness of love that is sweeter than life? It does not seem grievous to love to undergo a bitter death for the sake of her beloved.

Isaac's use of the symbolism of wine and inebriation is sometimes transformed into a eucharistic symbolism which is characteristic of the syriac tradition from Ephrem onwards. According to Isaac, love is food and drink, bread and wine, and these are at every hour given to those who love God:

When we find love, we partake of heavenly bread and are made strong without labour and toil. The heavenly bread is Christ, who came down from heaven and gave life to the world. This is the nourishment of the angels. The person who has found love eats and drinks Christ every day and every hour and is thereby made immortal. 'He that eateth of this bread', he says, 'which I will give him, shall not see death unto eternity.' Blessed is he who consumes the bread of love which is Jesus! He who eats love eats Christ, the God over all, as John bears witness saying, 'God is love'. … Love is the kingdom, where the Lord mystically promises his disciples [they will] eat in his kingdom. For when we hear him say, 'Ye shall eat and drink at the table of my kingdom', what do we suppose we shall eat, if not love? Love, rather than food and drink, is sufficient to nourish a man. This is the wine 'which maketh glad the heart of a man'. Blessed is he who partakes of this wine! Licentious men have drunk this wine and became chaste; sinners have drunk it and have forgotten the pathways of stumbling; drunkards have drunk this wine, and became fasters; the rich have drunk it and desired poverty; the poor have drunk it and been enriched with hope; the sick have drunk it and became strong; the unlearned have taken it and became wise.

7. FAITH AND KNOWLEDGE

The last theme we will consider in this chapter is Isaac's gnoseology, his teaching on the different kinds and degrees of knowledge, as well as on the interrelation between knowledge and faith. This constitutes, as it were, the theoretical background to his mysticism and must, thus, be analyzed within the context of his mystical teaching.

Faith and knowledge, Isaac claims, are two disparate paths. Acquiring faith presupposes silencing knowledge, and the increase of knowledge contributes to the extinguishing of faith:

The soul that by the pathways of discipline journeys on the road of faith often makes great progress therein. But if the soul returns once more to the ways of knowledge, she will straightway become lame in her faith and be bereft of faith's noetic force. … For the soul which in faith has surrendered herself to God once and for all, and has received through much experience the taste of his help, will not again take thought for herself. Nay rather, she is still in awestruck wonder and silence and has no power to return to the modes of her knowledge. … For knowledge is opposed to faith; but faith, in all that pertains to it, demolishes laws of knowledge—we do not, however, speak here of spiritual knowledge. For this is the definition of knowledge: that without investigation and examination it has no authority to do anything, but must investigate whether that which it considers and desires is possible. … But faith requires a mode of thinking that is single, limpidly pure, and simple, far removed from any deviousness.

… See how faith and knowledge are opposed to one another! The home of faith is a childlike thought and a simple heart. … But knowledge conspires against and opposes both these qualities. Knowledge in all its paths keeps within the boundaries of nature. But faith makes its journey above nature.

Faith, according to Isaac, possesses an unlimited creative potential, without being limited by the need to subject itself to natural laws. Knowledge, on the other hand, cannot act outside the limits of these laws. Knowledge, therefore, must serve nature with fear, whereas faith boldly goes beyond the limits of nature:

Fear accompanies knowledge, but confidence accompanies faith. The more a man journeys along the pathways of knowledge, the more he is shackled by fear and he cannot be found worthy of freedom from it. But a man who follows faith straightway becomes a free man and a ruler of himself, and a son of God with authority he freely weilds all things. The man who has found the keys of faith wields all the natures of creation even as God; for by faith comes the authority—after the likeness of God—to create a new creation. … And many times faith can bring everything forth from non-existence. But knowledge is unable to do anything without matter.

In this sense faith presupposes the possibility of a miracle, whereas knowledge excludes such a possibility as being outside the boundaries of natural law. The supernatural and miraculous character of faith is confirmed by the experience of christian martyrs and ascetics:

For it is by faith that men have entered into flames and bridled the burning power of the fire, walking unharmed through the midst thereof, and they have trodden upon the back of the sea as upon dry land. All these are above nature and opposed to the modes of knowledge. … The modes of knowledge governed the world for a little more or less than five thousand years, and man was not able in any wise to raise his head from the earth and perceive the power of his Creator. For this was not until our faith shone forth and freed us from the gloom of earthly labours … there is no knowledge that is not impoverished, however rich it should be; but heaven and earth cannot contain the treasures of faith.

While Isaac comes to the conclusion that faith is higher than knowledge, he concedes that faith and knowledge are not mutually exclusive. On the contrary, knowledge leads us to the threshold of faith, and faith draws knowledge to perfection:

Knowledge is perfected by faith and acquires the power to ascend on high, to perceive that which is higher than every perception and to see the radiance of him who is incomprehensible to the intellect and to the knowledge of created things. Knowledge is a step. By it a man can climb up to the lofty height of faith; and when a man has reached faith, he no longer has need of knowledge.

In spite of his emphasis on the superiority of faith over knowledge, Isaac was neither an adversary of rational knowledge nor a preacher of blind and intuitive faith. He regarded the way to God as a way passing not only from knowledge to faith, but also from faith to knowledge. In the first and second instances, the words 'faith' (haymanuta) and 'knowledge' (ida'ta) bear different connotations, however.

When Isaac speaks of the superiority of faith over knowledge, he emphasizes that faith is not only a matter of confessing certain dogmas: faith is an experience of encounter with divine reality. 'By faith,' Isaac says, we mean not that wherewith a man believes in the distinctions of the worshipful hypostases of the Divine Essence, in the properties of his nature, and in the wondrous dispensation to humankind through the assumption of our nature, though this faith, too, is very lofty. But we call faith that light which by grace dawns in the soul and fortifies the heart by the testimony of the mind, making it doubtfree through the assurance of the hope that is remote from all conceit. This faith manifests itself not by aural tradition, but with spiritual eyes it beholds the mysteries concealed in the soul, and the secret and divine riches that are hidden away from the eyes of the sons of flesh, but are unveiled by the Spirit to those who abide at Christ's table. ... The soul then rushes forward, despising every danger because of her trust in God, and on the wings of faith she soars aloft, taking leave of visible creation. She becomes as one drunken, in the awestruck wonder of her continual solicitude for God; and by simple, uncompounded vision, and by unseeing intuition concerning the Divine Nature, the intellect becomes accustomed to attending to rumination upon that nature's hiddenness.

The faith Isaac speaks of is an experiential awareness of God, an experience of the divine presence which he expresses in the terminology of 'inebriation', 'wonder' and 'vision'—his most characteristic mystical terminology. This faith is higher than any rational knowledge and it leads one beyond the limits of discursive reason. The term 'knowledge' in this context means that 'wisdom of this world' which is 'foolishness with God'. It is 'worldly knowledge' which leads one astray from God and it is in consequence opposed to faith.

'Worldly knowledge' is the first of the three degrees of knowledge described by Isaac. It is knowledge conducive to the progress of human civilization, science, and the arts. It is anthropocentric and atheistic knowledge. In its midst stands the arrogance of the human person who sees himself as a ruler of the universe:

When knowledge cleaves to the love of the body, it gathers up the following provisions: wealth, vainglory, honour, adornment, physical rest, special means of guarding the body's nature against adversities, assiduity in rational wisdom such as is suitable for the governance of the world and spews out the novelties of inventions, the arts, sciences, doctrines, and all things which crown the body in this world. Among the properties of this knowledge belong those that are opposed to faith. ... This is called shallow knowledge, for it is naked of all concern for God. And because it is dominated by the body, it introduces into the mind an irrational impotence, and its concern is totally for this world. ... It takes no account of God's providential governance, but, on the contrary, attributes every good thing in him to a man's diligence and his methods. ... The tree of the knowledge of good and evil, the tree that uproots love, is implanted in this very knowledge. ... In this knowledge are produced and are found presumption and pride, for it attributes every good thing to itself, and does not refer it to God.

Apart from 'shallow knowledge', however, there is a christian gnosis characterized by a striving to come to know God and to draw near him by observing the commandments and practising various forms of asceticism. This is the second degree of knowledge peculiar to a religious person who, in his ascent to God, has not yet attained perfection. When a person has reached this degree, he relies on 'fasting, prayer, mercy, reading of the divine Scripture, the modes of virtue, battle with the passions, and the rest'. Christian gnosis is a knowledge within the human soul which promotes faith but it is not itself the highest degree of knowledge:

This knowledge makes straight the pathways in the heart which lead to faith, wherewith we gather supplies for our journey to our true world. But even so, this knowledge is still corporeal and composite; and although it is the road that leads us and speeds us on our way toward faith, yet there remains the degree of knowledge still higher than this.

What, then, is this highest degree of knowledge? It is 'the degree of perfection' which totally surpasses the limits of rational knowledge and of ascetical efforts. It is that knowledge which is so swallowed up in the mystical experience of faith as to rise again with new capabilities:

When knowledge is raised above earthly things and the cares of earthly activities, and its thoughts begin to gain experience in inward matters which are hidden from the eyes,... and when it stretches itself upward and follows faith in its solicitude for the future age, in its desire for what has been promised us, and in searching deeply into hidden mysteries: then faith itself swallows up knowledge, converts it, and begets it anew, so that it becomes wholly and completely spirit. Then it can soar on wings in the realms of the bodiless and touch the depths of the unfathomable sea, musing upon the wondrous and divine workings of God's governance of noetic and corporeal creatures. It searches out spiritual mysteries that are perceived by the simple and subtle intellect. Then the inner senses awaken for spiritual doing, according to the order that will be in the immortal and incorruptible life. For even from now it has received, as it were in a mystery, the noetic resurrection as a true witness of the universal renewal of all things.

The highest spiritual state, which is born of faith, is the third degree of knowledge. Faith serves only as a way to this knowledge. The true knowledge attained by means of faith is the antithesis of 'worldly knowledge': the latter leads us astray from God; the former draws us closer to him; the latter is rational, the former mystical; the latter entails pride, the former, humility.

By humility true knowledge makes perfect the soul of those who have acquired it, like Moses, David, Isaiah, Peter, Paul, and the rest of the saints who have been accounted worthy of this perfect knowledge to the degree possible for human nature. And by diverse theorias and divine revelations, by the lofty vision of spiritual things and by ineffable mysteries and the like, their knowledge is swallowed up at all times, and in their own eyes they reckon their soul to be dust and ashes.

Notice how the mystical terminology of theoria, 'revelation', and 'vision' is now applied to knowledge, just as similar vocabulary was applied to faith in the passage quoted at the beginning of this section.

In the patristic tradition, the triple classification of knowledge is commonplace. Isaac himself refers to the teaching of 'Fathers' on natural, supra-natural, and contra-natural stages of knowledge. According to this classification, contra-natural knowledge refers to the atheistic knowledge that leads us astray from God, natural knowledge to the religious knowledge that leads us to God, and supra-natural, to the mystical knowledge that unites us with God.

The first degree of knowledge renders the soul cold to works that go in pursuit of good things. The second makes her fervent in the swift course on the level of faith. But the third is rest from labour, which is the type of the age to come, for the soul takes delight solely in the mind's meditation upon the mysteries of the good things to come.

Isaac does not always follow this traditional classification strictly. Sometimes he calls 'natural' any knowledge of the material world, 'spiritual', the knowledge of God, and 'supranatural', the knowledge of God and union with God. The last surpasses the limits of the term 'knowledge' and can be apophatically called 'unknowing', or 'supra-knowledge':

Knowledge that is occupied with visible things and receives instruction concerning them through the senses, is called natural. But knowledge that is occupied with the noetic power that is within things and with incorporeal natures is called spiritual. ... But that knowledge which is occupied with Divinity is called supra-natural, or rather, unknowing and knowledge-transcending.

The last two terms derive from the theological system of the Corpus Areopagiticum, where mystical knowledge of God is called 'unknowing'.

Isaac also employs a double classification of knowledge by distinguishing between 'natural' and 'spiritual' knowledge:

There is a knowledge that precedes faith, and there is a knowledge born of faith. Knowledge that precedes faith is natural knowledge; and that which is born of faith is spiritual knowledge.

Natural knowledge is a rational 'knowledge from below'; spiritual is supra-rational 'knowledge from above'. One should not think, emphasizes Isaac, that this supra-rational knowledge, this true communion with God, is accessible to philosophers' discursive way of thought:

Many simple people imagine that the philosophers' form of meditation is a foretaste of this converse that conveys the beauties of all of God's mysteries. The blessed Bishop Basil speaks of this in a latter to his brother, when he makes a distinction between this perception of creation that the saints receive—that is, the ladder of the intellect of which the blessed Evagrius spoke and being raised up above all ordinary vision—and the perception of the philosophers. 'There is', he says, 'a converse which opens up the door so that we can peer down into knowledge of created beings, and not up into spiritual meanings'. He is calling the philosophers' knowledge 'downwards knowledge', for, he says, even those who are subject to the passions can grasp this kind of knowledge; the perception which the saints receive through their intellect as a result of grace, however, he calls 'knowledge of the spiritual mysteries above'. Thus a person who is held worthy of this is in this condition night and day, like someone who has departed from the body and is already living in that world of the righteous. And this is the divine sweetness of which the pure-souled and wonderful Ammonius spoke: 'It is sweeter than honey and the honeycomb'—but not many solitaries and monks have known it. This is the entry into divine rest of which the Fathers spoke, and the crossing over from the regions of the passions to luminosity and to the stirrings of freedom.

Our attention is drawn in this passage by the abundance of patristic texts which are intended to confirm Isaac's ideas. In another passage in which he speaks of the two kinds of knowledge, Isaac refers to Mark the Ascetic and places knowledge in the context of ascetical practice:

There is one kind of knowledge, with its own strength, when this knowledge is occupied with virtue; but there is another kind of knowledge when this consists in the mind's reflection on God, just as the blessed Mark the Solitary said: 'There is one kind of knowledge which is concerned with objects, and another which is a knowledge of truth. Just as the sun is superior to the moon, so the second kind of knowledge is superior to and more advantageous than the first'. He calls 'knowledge concerned with objects' knowledge which is born from service and contests with the passions. ... Knowledge of truth, on the other hand, is knowledge ... resulting from the raising up of the intellect above everything, and from continual meditation on God, and by hope alone the intellect is raised through reflection to God.

The first kind of knowledge corresponds to what Greek-speaking authors, particularly Evagrius, called praktike (practice), while the second, to what they indicated by the term theoria (contemplation), the mystical ascent of the intellect to God.

True knowledge, according to Isaac, is the sense of the presence of God, a personal encounter with him, an experience of communion with divine reality. It gives birth to love and is a source of the highest sweetness:

Love is the offspring of knowledge, and knowledge is the offspring of the health of the soul... .

Question: What is knowledge?

Answer: The perception of life immortal.

Question: And what is life immortal?

Answer: Consciousness in God. [For love comes from knowledge, and] knowledge concerning God is king of all desires and every sweetness of the earth is superfluous to the heart that has received it. For there is nothing which can be likened to the sweetness of the knowledge of God.

No one can obtain true knowledge until he reaches purity of mind, childlike simplicity, and sanctity. To receive spiritual knowledge, one has to renounce human knowledge:

Not only it is impossible for ... spiritual knowledge to be received by this merely human knowledge, but not even an inkling of it can be perceived by those who are zealous in training themselves in such knowledge. And if any of these men should wish to approach the knowledge of the spirit, then until they repudiate human knowledge ... and establish themselves in a childlike manner of thought, they will not be able to draw near it, not even by a little. ... Spiritual knowledge is simple and does not shine upon human conceptions. Until our mind has been freed from its many conceptions and enters the unified simplicity of purity, it can never experience spiritual knowledge. ... A man cannot receive spiritual knowledge except he be converted, and becomes as a little child. For only then does he experience that delight which belongs to the kingdom of the heavens. By 'kingdom of the heavens' the Scriptures mean spiritual contemplation.

Spiritual knowledge cannot be acquired through human efforts: it is a gift from God. It does not come as a direct consequence of virtuous living, nor is it derived from virtues, though it is given as a reward for virtues. Spiritual knowledge leads one to the highest degree of faith which is no longer a 'faith by hearing', but 'confidence of things hoped for, the evidence of things not seen'. Spiritual knowledge is a gift which comes from repentance, says Isaac.

Concerning this we have written, 'That of which we have received an earnest by baptism, we receive as a gift by means of repentance'... . Spiritual knowledge is the perception of what is hidden. And when a man perceives these invisible and by far more excellent things, from which it takes the name spiritual knowledge, then there is begotten by the perception proper to this knowledge another faith, not one which is opposed to the first faith, but one which confirms it. And this is called 'the faith of divine vision (te'orya)'. Until then, hearing; but now, divine vision. But contemplation is more certain than hearing.

By now it should be clear that by various ways Isaac comes to the same conclusion: the pinnacle of the spiritual life is mystical experience, whatever name may be applied to it—spiritual prayer, contemplation, revelation, vision, illumination, insight, faith of contemplation, spiritual knowledge. The path to this experience may be described as a way from praktike to theoria, from hearing to vision, from darkness to illumination, from rational knowledge to supra-rational faith, from intuitive faith to spiritual knowledge, from 'worldly knowledge' to 'divine unknowing' or 'supra-knowledge'. The way is endless. It will reach culmination only in the age to come, when one reaches contemplation and the knowledge of God to the greatest extent:

… Before a man can approach knowledge he must ascend and descend in his manner of life; but when he actually draws nigh to knowledge, he is altogether raised on high. However much he is exalted, his ascent in knowledge will not be completed until the age of glory comes, and then he will receive the full measure of his riches.

———————————

CHAPTER VIII

THE LIFE OF THE AGE TO COME

I am of the opinion that he is going to manifest some wonderful outcome, a matter of immense and ineffable compassion on the part of the glorious Creator ...II/39,6

God is not One who requites evil, but he sets evil aright.

II/39,15

The majority of humankind will enter the kingdom of heaven without the experience of gehenna.

II/40,12

THE LAST THEME in our investigation into the thought of Saint Isaac the Syrian is his eschatology. It is an integral part of his theological system and derives from his conviction that God is love. Although based upon his own mystical insights, Isaac's eschatological ideas are confirmed by the authority of earlier Church Fathers.

The traditional monastic themes of the 'meditation on the future world' and the 'remembrance of death' begin this chapter. In the second section we shall collect Isaac's eschatological opinions which are spread throughout the corpus of his writings, excluding Chapters XXXIX and XL of Part II. As these two chapters (together with Chapter XLI) contain a systematic treatment of specifically eschatological themes, it seems appropriate to analyze them in the two concluding sections of this chapter.

1. MEDITATION ON THE FUTURE WORLD

The monastic tradition of the Christian East assigns great value to the 'remembrance of death'. 'Always remember your departure and do not be forgetful of eternal judgment', advises Evagrius. 'Each day have death before your eyes. ... Prepare yourself for the fearful day of answering on the Judgment of God', repeats Abba Isaias the Solitary. In the syriac tradition, the themes of remembrance of death and the Last Judgment are developed by Saint Ephrem, one of whose eschatological texts Isaac quotes in the following passage:

So long as we are in this world, God does not affix his seal either to what is good or to what is evil, even up to the moment of our departure. ... And as Saint Ephrem says, we should make our soul like a ready ship that does not know when a favourable wind will blow, or like a tenant who does not know when the landlord will give the order to depart. And if, he says, merchants are so well prepared for the sake of a little gain, though they may perhaps return soon from their voyage, how much more should we make ourselves ready, and prepare ourselves in advance, before the coming of that decisive day, that bridge and door into the new age?

The transitory character of human nature, according to Isaac, is the first thought which descends from God into a human person and creates in him a good foundation for the way leading to profound contemplation. Every evening, before sleeping, one should remind oneself of death, imagining that this night may be his last:

When you approach to your bed, say to it, 'This very night, perchance, you will be my tomb, O bed; for I know not whether tonight instead of a transient sleep, the eternal sleep of death will be mine'.

It is necessary always to remember the Last Judgment, and to prepare oneself to encounter God:

What is concern over God's Judgment? It is: a continual quest after his rest; mourning at all times and a contrite meditation on account of those things which always remain imperfect because of the wretchedness of our nature; constant sadness on their account which the mind retains through powerful thoughts and which in prayer it offers up before God as an offering with humble compunction; and, inasmuch as it is possible and is within a man's power, to hold solicitude for the body in disdain. Such is the man who carries in his soul the continuous memory of God. As Saint Basil says, 'Undistracted prayer is that which produces in the soul a distinct reflection on God. And God's indwelling is this: to have God established in us by unceasing memory of him'. In this manner we become temples of God.

Remembrance of death and the age to come helps us overcome our fear of death:

As long as a man chooses to be free of possessions, departure from this life always arises in his mind. He makes the life after the resurrection his continual study, and at all times he contrives to make preparation that will be useful yonder. ... He does not even fear death itself, because his attention is always upon it, as something that approaches him, and he awaits it.

Remembrance of the Last Judgment, which occurs to a person as a result of spiritual illumination, is conducive to his progress to spiritual perfection. Remembering his last hour, he becomes more collected and attentive to his deeds:

When the faculty of reason begins to become illumined in us, fear of death is completely scorned, and a person is continually stirred by expectation of the resurrection, ... concern over divine judgment is strong in that person, and he begins night and day to examine his manner of life, his words and his thoughts; and if he conducts himself in all sorts of good ways and fine manners of labours, then this concern and recollection is never far removed from him.

'Reflection upon the restitution to come' must be a constant activity of an ascetic. Isaac cites as an example a monk who, during his prayer, reflects upon eschatological matters:

How did God bring creation ... out of non-being into being? And how will he again cause creation to perish from its wondrous harmony, the beauty of nature and the well-ordered course of its creatures: times and seasons, the union of night and day, the beneficial changes of the year, the many-hued flowers of the earth, the beautiful buildings of the cities, their magnificent palaces, the swift course of men and their nature which endures hardship from its beginning in life till its departure? How will he suddenly abolish this wondrous order and establish another age, wherein the memory of the former creation will never again enter into the heart of any man, but a change of another thought will come to pass, and other deliberations, other concerns?

And Isaac continues:

The human nature will in no wise remember the world of the way of life which was therein. For the gaze of man's mind will be held in bondage by the vision of that state and it will never again have time to turn back in recollection to the conflict with flesh and blood. At the destruction of that former age, the future age will commence straightway.

This prayerful meditation leads the ascetic to the state of wonder at the greatness of God:

Once someone has stood amazed, and filled his intellect with the majesty of God, amazed at all these things he has done and is doing, then he wonders in astonishment at his mercifulness, how, after all these things, God has prepared for them another world that has no end, whose glory is not even revealed to the angels, even though they are involved in his activities insofar as is possible in the life of the spirit, in accordance with the gift with which their nature has been endowed. That person wonders too at how excelling is that glory, and how exalted is the manner of existence at that time; and how insignificant is the present life compared to what is reserved for creation in the New Life... .

Eschatological meditation on the things of the future age is a source of spiritual rebirth and renewal. It gradually extinguishes all bodily cares, replacing them with thoughts of the age to come:

The beginning of the renewal of the inner person consists, then, in meditation and constant reflection on the things to come. By this means the person is little by little purified of customary distraction on earthly things: he becomes like a snake which has sloughed off its old skin, and is renewed and rejuvenated. Similarly, inasmuch as bodily thoughts, and concern for these, diminish in the mind, accordingly reflection on things heavenly, and the gazing on things to come, increasingly springs up in the soul. Delight in the ministry of these things overcomes and proves stronger than the pleasure of the bodily thoughts.

2. LIFE AFTER DEATH

To highlight the main elements of Isaac's views on christian eschatology we shall look at the passages where he speaks of death and the resurrection of the dead, of the separation of the righteous from the sinners, and of the torment of gehenna and the blessing of paradise.

By Isaac's decription, death is that blessed Sabbath when human nature rests on the eve of its final resurrection:

Six days are accomplished in the husbandry of life by means of keeping the commandments; the seventh is spent entirely in the grave; and the eight is in departure from it. ... The true Sabbath, the Sabbath that is not a similitude, is the tomb, which reveals and manifests perfect repose from the tribulations of the passions and from the toil against them. The whole man, both soul and body, then keeps the Sabbath.

Understanding the Sabbath as a symbol of death is very traditional: we find it in both patristic literature and liturgical texts. No less traditional is the interpretation of the eighth day as a symbol of the resurrection. According to Isaac, the bodily resurrection of the age to come is also symbolized by the resurrection of the body from sin during earthly life:

The true resurrection of the body is when it receives that ineffable transformation in that future state, at the stripping off of all fleshly refuse and what belongs to it. The symbolic resurrection of the body is when it rises from all the sin to which it was attached in its activity, and applies itself to the excellent practice of service to God.

The Last Judgment is the moment of the human person's encounter, not only with God, but also with the people with whom he was linked during his earthly life. The sentence of the Judge will mean that a person either enters into the kingdom of Christ together with the righteous, or is separated from them. This sentence will do no more than confirm the state reached by that person during his life. Somone who was separated from his fellows by his sinful life will be separated from them in the life to come:

Woe to that monk who has proven false to his vow, who, trampling upon his conscience, stretches forth his hand to the devil! ... With what countenance will he meet the Judge when his companions who have attained purity will greet one another? For he had parted ways with them and walked the path of perdition. ... But what is more terrible, just as he has separated his path from theirs, so Christ will separate him from them in that day when the shining cloud will bear upon its back their bodies made resplendent by purity and carry them through the gates of heaven.

The life of the age to come is, in Isaac, 'a continual and ineffable rest in God'. It is characterized by the absence of 'bodily actions', which are replaced by the mind's reflection, the 'delightful gaze and vision without distraction'. The mind of a person in the age to come will be occupied with the contemplation of God's beauty in the state of wonder:

There human nature never ceases from its awestruck wonder at God. ... But since all the beauty of things to exist in the newness to come is inferior to his beauty, how can the intellect depart from the beauty of God in its contemplation?

In the future age, the hierarchical order of the universe through which revelations devolve from God to the higher ranks of angels, and from them to the lower ranks and to the humankind, will no longer have any place:

In the future age ... this order of things will be abolished. For then one will not receive from another the revelation of God's glory to the gladness and joy of his soul; but to each by himself the Master will give according to the measure of his excellence and his worthiness, and he will not receive the gift from his comrade as he does here. Then there will be no teacher and no pupil, nor one whose deficiency must be filled up by another. For one is the Giver there, who gives without mediation to those who receive; and those who win joy, procure it from him. ... There the order of those who teach and those who learn ceases, and on One alone hangs the ardent love of all.

Nobody can enter in future blessing by compulsion: everyone has to make his own choice for God. Once made, this choice is manifested in the present life in the rejection of the passions and in repentance:

It is not a case of the created beings' inheriting the glory to come by compulsion or against a person's will, without any repentance being involved; rather, it so pleased his wisdom that they should choose the good out of the volition of their own free will, and thus have a way of coming to him.

Future blessing will be the lot of those who during their life have reached 'the land of promise' and united themselves with God. Yet Isaac does not exclude from the kingdom of heaven those who, without having seen this land close at hand, died in the hope of attaining it. Those who hoped to reach perfection, but did not, will be added to the Old Testament righteous who never saw Christ in their lifetimes, but died in the hope of seeing him.

Those who enter the kingdom of heaven will find themselves in varying degrees of closeness to God, each in accordance with his capacity for accommodating the light of the Godhead. Even so, a difference in degree will not involve hierarchical inequality among those who have been saved, and no one will be inferior to the other:

The Saviour calls the 'many mansions' of his Father's house the noetic levels of those who dwell in that land, that is, the distinctions of the gifts and the spiritual degrees which they noetically take delight in, as well as the diversity of the ranks of the gifts. But by this he did not mean that each person yonder will be confined in his existence by a separate spatial dwelling and by the manifest, distinguishing mark of the diverse placement of each man's abode. Rather, it resembles how each one of us derives a unique benefit from this visible sun though a single enjoyment of it common to all, each according to the clarity of his eyesight and the ability of his pupils to contain the sun's constant effusion of light. ... In the same manner, those who at the appointed time will be deemed worthy of that realm will dwell in one abode which will not be divided into a multitude of separate parts. And according to the rank of his discipline each man draws delight for himself from the one noetic Sun in one air, one place, one dwelling, one vision, and one outward appearance. He whose measure is less will not see the great measure of his neighbour's rank, lest he should think that this arises from the multitude of his neighbour's gifts and the fewness of his own, and this very thing should become for him a cause of sadness and mental anguish. Far be it that one should suppose such a thing to occur in that realm of delights! Each man inwardly takes delight in the gift and the lofty rank whereof he has been deemed worthy.

Though there are many mansions in the kingdom of heaven, none is to be found anywhere except inside that kingdom. Beyond its borders, there is only gehenna. Isaac was not aware of any other intermediate state between these two realms:

In the future separation there will be no middle realm between the state that is completely on high and the state that is absolutely below. A person will either belong entirely to those who dwell on high, or entirely to those below; but within both the one state and the other are diverse degrees of recompense. If this is true, which it most certainly is, what is more senseless and more foolish than those who say that 'It is enough for me to escape gehenna, I do not seek to enter into the kingdom'! For to escape gehenna means precisely to enter the kingdom, even as falling away from the kingdom is entering gehenna. Scripture has taught us nothing about the existence of three realms, but 'When the Son of God will come in his glory, he shall set the sheep on his right hand, but the goats on the left'. [Other references to the Gospel follow at this point.]... . How have you not understood by these things that falling short of the order on high is, in fact, the gehenna of torment?

What, then, are paradise and gehenna in Isaac's vision? The blessing of paradise, according to him, is human persons' participation in the love of God—itself 'the tree of life' and 'the heavenly bread':

Paradise is the love of God, wherein is the enjoyment of all blessedness, and there the blessed Paul partook of supernatural nourishment. When he tasted there of the tree of life, he cried out, saying, 'Eye hath not seen, nor ear heard, neither have entered into the heart of man, the things which God hath prepared for them that love him'. Adam was barred from this tree through the devil's counsel. The tree of life is the love of God from which Adam fell away. ... When we find love, we partake of heavenly bread. ... The heavenly bread is Christ, who came down from heaven and gave life to the world... . Therefore, the man who lives in love reaps the fruit of life from God, and while yet in this world, he even now breathes the air of the resurrection; in this air the righteous will delight in the resurrection.

The torment of gehenna, in Isaac's vision, is constituted by a human person's inability to participate in the love of God.

This does not mean that sinners in gehenna are deprived of the love of God. On the contrary, this love is given to everyone equally, both to the righteous and to sinners. But for the former it becomes a source of delight and blessedness in paradise; for the latter it is a source of torment:

I also maintain that those who are punished in gehenna are scourged by the scourge of love. Nay, what is so bitter and vehement as the torment of love? I mean that those who have become conscious that they have sinned against love suffer greater torment from this than from any fear of punishment. For the sorrow caused in the heart by sin against love is more poignant than any torment. It would be improper for a man to think that sinners in gehenna are deprived of the love of God. Love ... is given to all. But the power of love works in two ways: it torments sinners, even as happens here when a friend suffers from a friend; but it becomes a source of joy for those who have observed its duties. Thus I say that this is the torment of gehenna: bitter regret. But love inebriates the souls of the sons of heaven by its delectability.

While Isaac, following the Gospel text, believes that on the Day of Judgment, the sheep will be separated from the goats, and that the goats will be sent to gehenna, this belief does not preclude hope in God's mercy, which, in his view, surpasses every human idea of a just requital. This hope in God's mercifulness leads Isaac to conclude that the torment of gehenna cannot be eternal. If evil, sin, death, and gehenna do not have their origins in God, how can one presume that they will be eternal? If the devil and demons, as well as all evil people, were created by God as good and sinless, but by their own free choice fell away from God, how can one suppose that God will eternally reconcile himself with this situation? These questions were raised long before Isaac by several Fathers and teachers of the Church, notably by Origen and Gregory of Nyssa.

One of the Homilies in Part I which was not translated into Greek is entitled 'Against those who say: If God is good, for what reason has he made these things?' In this homily Isaac opposes a dualistic understanding of the co-eternal existence of good and evil, God and the devil. In this dialectic, Isaac bases himself on a teaching commonly accepted in christian tradition, that God is not the creator of evil and thus evil has no substantial existence. 'Sin, gehenna, and death do not exist at all with God, for they are effects, not substances,' Isaac says.

Sin is the fruit of free will. There was a time when sin did not exist, and there will be a time when it will not exist. Gehenna is the fruit of sin. At some point in time it had a beginning, but its end is not known. Death, however, is a dispensation of the wisdom of the Creator. It will rule only a short time over nature; then it will be totally abolished. Satan's name derives from voluntary turning aside from the truth; it is not an indication that he exists as such naturally.

Therefore, according to Isaac, sin, death, and gehenna will be abolished by God, though the end of gehenna is a mystery which goes beyond human understanding and also beyond the dogmatic teaching of the Church. Isaac does not choose to develop here the notion of a non-eternal gehenna, but simply implies that at some time it will be abolished. His attention is riveted not so much on gehenna as on the future existence of the transfigured universe which will take place after gehenna's annihilation.

Isaac's eschatological vision is replete with optimism. In this it is close to the eschatology of Saint Paul, who speaks of the final transfiguration of the whole creation, when death will be 'swallowed up by victory' and God will be 'all in all'. Isaac was thoroughly convinced that this promise will be fulfilled, even though there will be a preceding period when sinners will be tormented in gehenna. Hope in the final transfiguration of all being evoked in Isaac a hymn of thanksgiving to God, whose mercy has no limits:

O the astonishment at the goodness of our God and Creator! O might for which all is possible! O the immeasurable kindness toward our nature, that he will bring even sinners back into existence! Who is able to glorify him? He raises up the transgressor and blasphemer. ... Where is gehenna, that can afflict us? Where is the torment that terrifies us in many ways and quenches the joy of his love? And what is gehenna compared with the grace of his resurrection, when he will raise us from sheol and cause our corruptible nature to be clad in incorruption, and raise up in glory what has fallen into sheol? Come, men of discernment, and be filled with wonder! Whose mind is sufficiently wise to wonder worthily at the bounty of our Creator? His recompense to sinners is that, instead of a just recompense, he rewards them with resurrection, and instead of those bodies with which they trampled upon his law, he robes them with the glory of perfection. That grace whereby we are resurrected after we have sinned is greater than the grace which brought us into being when we were not, O Lord! Behold, Lord, the waves of thy grace close my mouth in silence, and there is not a thought left in me, not even for giving thanks to thee. ... Glory be to thee for the two worlds which thou hast created for our growth and delight... .

3. ETERNAL PUNISHMENT OR UNIVERSAL SALVATION?

The lot of human beings after death became an object of Isaac's special attention in the three concluding chapters of Part II. In Chapter XXXIX, called 'Contemplation on the theme of gehenna, in so far as grace can be granted to human nature to hold opinions on these mysteries', he includes a detailed discussion, with references to preceding Fathers, on the nature, aim, and duration of the torments of gehenna. This is continued in Chapter XL, where he develops the same sort of ideas while laying special emphasis on the love of God. Finally, in Chapter XLI, he presents the moral conclusions that derive from the two preceding chapters.

The discussion begins in Chapter XXXIX with the question of the purpose for the establishment of gehenna. Isaac emphasizes that God does nothing out of retribution: even to think this way about God would be blasphemous. This opinion is all the more unacceptable in view of God's foreknowledge that humanity would sin and fall even before he created human beings, yet still he created them:

To suppose that retribution for evil acts is to be found in him is abominable. By implying that he makes use of such a great and difficult thing out of retribution we are attributing a weakness to the Divine Nature. We cannot even believe such a thing can be found in those human beings who live a virtuous and upright life and whose thoughts are entirely in accord with the divine will—let alone believe of God that he has done something out of retribution for anticipated evil acts in connection with those whose nature he has brought into being with honour and great love. Knowing them and all their conduct, the flow of his grace did not dry up from them: not even after they started living amid many evil deeds did he withhold his care for them, even for a moment.

Still worse is the opinion that God allows people to lead sinful lives on earth in order to punish them eternally after death.

If someone says that [God] has put up with them here on earth in order that his patience may be known—with the idea that he would later punish them mercilessly—such a person thinks in an unspeakably blasphemous way about God because of his infantile way of thinking: he is removing from God his kindness, goodness, and compassion: all the things because of which he truly bears with sinners and wicked men. Such a person is attributing to God enslavement to passion, imagining that he has not consented to their being chastised here with a view to a much greater misfortune he has prepared for them, in exchange for a short-lived patience. Not only does such a person fail to attribute something praiseworthy to God, but he also calumniates him.

'A right way of thinking about God', according to Isaac, rejects the view that 'weakness, or passibility, or whatever else might be involved in the course of retribution' has anything to do with God. On the contrary, all of God's actions 'are directed towards the single eternal good, whether each receives judgment or something of glory from Him—not by way of retribution, far from it!—but with a view to the advantage that is going to come from all these things'.

Within the context of God's kindness and mercy, Isaac refers to the biblical story of the damnation of Adam and Eve for the sin they committed, and of their exile from paradise. Though the establishment of death and exile were decreed under the guise of damnation, it concealed a blessing:

Just as [God] decreed death, under the appearance of a sentence, for Adam because of sin, and just as he showed by means of the punishment that the sin existed—even so this punishment was not his real aim. He showed it as something Adam would receive as a repayment for his wrong, but he hid its true mystery, and under the guise of something to be feared he concealed his eternal intention concerning death and what his wisdom was aiming at. Even though this matter might be grievous, ignominious, and hard at first, nevertheless in truth it would be the means of transporting us to that wonderful and glorious world. Without it, there would be no way of crossing over from this world and being there. ... The Creator did not say: 'This will turn out to be the cause of good things to come for you and a life more glorious than this'. Instead, he showed it as something which would bring about our misfortune and dissolution. Again, when he expelled Adam and Eve from paradise, he expelled them under the outward aspect of anger ... as though dwelling in paradise had been taken away from them because they were unworthy. But within all this rested the divine plan, fulfilling and guiding everything towards what had been the Creator's original intention from the beginning. It was not disobedience which introduced death to the house of Adam, nor did transgression remove them from paradise, for it is clear that God did not create Adam and Eve to be in Paradise, just a small portion of the earth; rather, they were going to subjugate the entire earth. For this reason we do not even say that he removed them because of the commandment which had been transgressed; for it is not the case that, had they not transgressed the commandment, they would have been left in paradise for ever.

Therefore, contrary to widespread opinion, Isaac considered death a blessing in that it intrinsically contains the potential of future resurrection; and the exile from paradise as beneficial, since instead of receiving a 'small portion of the earth', humankind was given all of creation as its possession. This approach to the biblical text is based on the exegetical tradition of Theodore of Mopsuestia, according to whom death was profitable for human beings because it opened to them a way to repentance and restoration.

In the establishment of death, God's 'cunning' was revealed: he concealed his true intention under the guise of punishment for sin. The same 'cunning' explains the establishment of gehenna as a punishment whose aim is the profit which humans may derive from it:

You should see that, while God's caring is guiding us all the time to what he wishes for us, as things outwardly appear, it is from us that he takes the occasion to providing things, his aim being to carry out by every means what he has intended for our advantage. All this is because he knew beforehand our inclination towards all sorts of wickedness, and so he cunningly made the harmful consequences which would result from this into a means of entry to the future good and the setting right of our corrupted state. These are things which are known only to him. But after we have been exercised and assisted little by little as a result of these consequences after they have occurred, we realize and perceive that it could not turn out otherwise than in accordance with what has been foreseen by him. This is how everything works with him, even though things may seem otherwise to us: with him it is not a matter of retribution, but he is always looking beyond to the advantage that will come from his dealings with humanity. And one such thing is the matter of gehenna.

Thus Isaac gradually arrives at his key idea: the final outcome of the history of the universe must correspond to the majesty of God, and the final destiny of human beings should be worthy of God's mercifulness. 'I am of the opinion', Isaac claims,

that he is going to manifest some wonderful outcome, a matter of immense and ineffable compassion on the part of the glorious Creator, with respect to the ordering of this difficult matter of gehenna's torment: out of it the wealth of his love and power and wisdom will become known all the more—and so will the insistent might of the waves of his goodness. It is not the way of the compassionate Maker to create rational beings in order to deliver them over mercilessly to unending affliction in punishment for things of which he knew even before they were fashioned, aware how they would turn out when he created them—and whom nonetheless he created. All the more since the foreplanning of evil and the taking of vengeance are characteristic of the passions of created beings, and do not belong to the Creator. For all this characterizes people who do not know or who are unaware of what they are doing ... for as a result of some matter that has occurred unexpectedly to them they are incited by the vehemence of anger to take vengeance. Such action does not belong to the Creator who, even before the cycle of the depiction of creation has been portrayed, knew of all that was before and all that was after in connection with the actions and intentions of rational beings.

To confirm these ideas, Isaac refers to Theodore of Mopsuestia's teaching on the torment that is not unending, and to Diodore of Tarsus' ideas that torment will last only a short time, whereas the blessing is for all eternity, and that 'not even the immense wickedness of the demons can overcome the measure of God's goodness'.

'These and similar astounding insights and opinions leading us on to love of and wonder at the Creator', Isaac comments with enthusiasm,belong to these very pillars of the Church. … Such opinions will cast away from our way of thinking the childish opinion of God expressed by those who introduce evil and passibility into his nature, saying that he is changed by circumstances and times. At the same time these opinions [of Theodore and Diodore] will teach us about the nature of his chastisements and punishments, whether here or there, instructing us concerning what sort of compassionate intentions and purpose he has in allowing these to come upon us, what are the excellent outcomes resulting from them, how it is not a matter of our being destroyed by them or enduring the same for eternity, how he allows them to come in a fatherly way, and not vengefully—which would be a sign of hatred. Their purpose was that, by thinking in this way, we might come to know about God, and wonder at him would draw us to love of him, and as a result of that love we might feel ashamed at ourselves and set aright the conduct of our lives here.

Isaac did not think that the end of torment would lead to laxity and the loss of the fear of God. Quite the contrary. This idea, according to him, incites within a person love of God and the repentance that comes from the measureless mercy of the Creator. The thought of God as a caring Father gives birth in a person to a filial love for, and adherence to, him, whereas the notion of God as a chastiser can only cause a slavish fear and dread before him.

All the afflictions and sufferings which fall to someone's lot are sent from God with the aim of bringing a person to an inner change. Isaac draws an important conclusion: God never retaliates for the past, but always cares for our future. 'All kinds and manner of chastisements and punishments that come from him,' Isaac suggests,

are not brought about in order to requite past actions, but for the sake of the subsequent gain to be gotten in them. … This is what the Scriptures bring to our attention and remind us of,… that God is not One who requites evil, but who sets evil aright: the one is characteristic of evil people, while the other is characteristic of a father. Scripture shows him as if he were bringing good and evil by way of requital, whereas his purpose is not in fact this, but instilling in us love and awe. … If this were not the case, what resemblance does Christ's coming have with the deeds of the generations which were prior to it? Does this immense compassion seem to you to be a retribution for those evil deeds? Tell me, if God is someone who requites evil, and he does what he does by means of requital, what commensurate requital do you see here, O man?

The idea of love contradicts the idea of requital, Isaac insists. Besides, if we were to suppose that God will punish sinners eternally, this would mean that the creation of the world was a mistake, that God proved unable to oppose evil, which is not within his will. If we ascribe requital to God's actions, we apply weakness to God:

So then, let us not attribute to God's actions and his dealings with us any idea of requital. Rather, we should speak of fatherly provision, a wise dispensation, a perfect will which is concerned with our good, and complete love.

If it is a case of love, then it is not one of requital; and if it is a case of requital, then it is not one of love. Love, when it operates, is not concerned with the requiting of former things by means of its own good deeds or correction; rather, it looks to what is most advantageous in the future: it examines what is to come, and not things of the past. If we think otherwise than this, then according to the resulting childish view the Creator will prove to be weak ... for after what he had established had become corrupted against his will, he devised some other plan, preparing ills in return for its corruption. Such are the feeble ways of understanding the Creator!

All of God's actions are mysteries inaccessible to human reasoning. Gehenna is also a mystery, created in order to bring to a state of perfection those who had not reached it during their lifetime:

In the matter of the afflictions and sentence of gehenna, there is some hidden mystery whereby the wise Maker has taken as a starting point for its future outcome the wickedness of our actions and willfulness, using it as a way of bringing to perfection his dispensation, wherein lies the teaching which makes one wise, and the advantage beyond description, hidden from both angels and human beings, hidden too from those who are being chastised, whether they be demons or human beings, hidden for as long as the ordained period of time holds sway.

Gehenna, then, is a sort of purgatory rather than hell: it is conceived and established for the salvation of both human beings and fallen angels. Yet this true aim of gehenna is hidden from those who are chastised in it, and will be revealed only after gehenna is abolished.

Isaac then returns to his earlier statement that requital does not correspond to God's goodness. In doing so he advances the following logical considerations that oppose this idea:

One speaks of requital when he who is the requiter is gradually instructed about the requital needed as a result of, and corresponding to, the good and bad actions that take place: along with actions which differ from day to day, he acquires a different knowledge, and his consequent thoughts are subject to outside causes and take their origin from temporal circumstances. If the kingdom and gehenna had not been foreseen in the purpose of our good God ... then God's thoughts concerning them would not be eternal. But righteousness and sin were known by him before they revealed themselves. Accordingly the kingdom and gehenna are matters belonging to mercy; they were conceived of in their essence by God as a result of his eternal goodness. It was not a matter of requiting, even though he gave them the name of requital. That we should further say or think that the matter is not full of love and mingled with compassion would be an opinion laden with blasphemy and an insult to our Lord God. By saying that he will even hand us over to burning for the sake of sufferings, torment, and all sorts of ills, we are attributing to the Divine Nature an enmity towards the very rational beings which he created through grace; the same is true if we say that he acts or thinks with spite and with a vengeful purpose, as though he were avenging himself.

As we have seen, Isaac used every possible source to support his teaching on the incompatibility of an eternal gehenna with God's love and goodness: Scripture, patristic writings, and finally logical considerations. As we saw in Chapter I, the conviction that God is love was the driving force behind Isaac's whole theological system. Now we observe the seal this conviction placed on his eschatology.

4. DIVINE LOVE WHICH REVEALS ITSELF IN THE FINAL DESTINY OF THE WORLD

The theme of God's boundless love, begun in Chapter XXXIX of Part II, continues to be developed in Chapter XL, which is dedicated to 'the constancy, harmony and love of the divine nature at both the beginning and at the end of creation'. Here Isaac claims that the love God has for his creatures does not change because of changes that happen with them. From very eternity, God is one and the same in what belongs to him by nature: 'there exists with him a single love and compassion which is spread out over all creation, a love which is without alteration, timeless and everlasting'.

The state of having turned away from God is unnatural, according to Isaac, and God will not permit those who withdrew from him to remain in this state for ever: he will bring to salvation all those who have fallen away. But this salvation will not be forced upon anyone: each person will turn to God of his own free will when he reaches the state of maturity. The purpose for which God brought creatures into the world remains the same whatever way they have chosen for themselves; sooner or later they will be brought to salvation. For Isaac, the final salvation of those who have fallen, including all sinners and demons, is a necessity:

It is clear that [God] does not abandon them the moment they fall, and that demons will not remain in their demonic state, and sinners will not remain in their sins; rather, he is going to bring them to a single equal state of perfection in relationship to his own Being—to a state in which the holy angels now are, in perfection of love and a passionless mind. He is going to bring them into that excellency of will where it will be not as though they were curbed and not free or having stirrings from the Opponent then; rather, they will be in a state of excelling knowledge, with a mind made mature in the stirrings which partake of the divine outpouring which the blessed Creator is preparing in his grace; they will be perfected in love for him, with a perfect mind which is above any aberration in all its stirrings.

All those who have fallen away from God will eventually return to him because of temporary, short torment in gehenna that has been prepared for them so that they may purify themselves through the fire of suffering and repentance. Having passed through this purification by fire, they will attain to the angelic state.

Maybe they will be raised to a perfection even greater than that in which the angels now exist; for all are going to exist in a single love, a single purpose, a single will, and a single perfect state of knowledge; they will gaze towards God with the desire of insatiable love, even if some divine dispensation [i.e. gehenna] may in the meantime be effected for reasons known to God alone, lasting for a fixed period, decreed by him in accordance with the will of his wisdom.

God does not forget any of his creatures. Every human being has a place reserved for him in the kingdom of heaven. For those who are unable to enter immediately into the kingdom, the transitory period of gehenna has been established:

No part belonging to any single one of all rational beings will be lost, so far as God is concerned, in the preparation of that supernal kingdom which is prepared for all worlds. Because of the goodness of his nature by which he brought the universe into being and then bears, guides, and provides for the worlds and all created things in his immeasurable compassion, he has devised the establishment of the kingdom of heaven for the entire community of rational beings—even though an intervening time is reserved for the general raising of all beings to the same level. And we say this so that we too may concur with the magisterial teaching of Scripture. Nevertheless gehenna is grievous, even if it is thus limited in its extent: who can possibly bear it? For this reason the angels in heaven rejoice at a single sinner who repents.

If a genuine righteousness were required of human beings, then only one in ten thousand would be able to enter the kingdom of heaven, continues Isaac. This is why God gave people repentance as a remedy, for it can heal a person from sin in a short time. Not wishing human beings to perish, God forgives everyone who repents with his whole heart. God is good by nature, and he 'wishes to save everyone by all sorts of means'.

Isaac resented the widespread opinion that the majority of human beings will be punished in hell, while only a small group of the chosen will delight in paradise. He was convinced that, quite the contrary, the majority of people will find themselves in the kingdom of heaven, and only a few sinners will go to gehenna, and even they only for the period of time necessary for their repentance and remission of sins:

By the device of grace the majority of humankind will enter the kingdom of heaven without the experience of gehenna. But this is apart from those who, because of their hardness of heart and utter abandonment to wickedness and the lusts, fail to show remorse in suffering for their faults and their sins, and because these people have not been disciplined at all. For God's holy nature is so good and so compassionate that it is always seeking to find some small means of putting us in the right: how he can forgive human beings their sins—like the case of the tax collector who was put in the right by the intensity of his prayer or like the case of a woman with two small coins or the man who received forgiveness on the cross. For God wishes our salvation, and not reasons to torment us.

Earthly life is given to everyone as a time of repentance. It is enough for a person to turn to God to ask forgiveness for his sins immediately to be forgiven. The token of this forgiveness is the Incarnation of the Word of God, who, when all creation had abandoned and forgotten God, came down to earth in order to redeem humankind and the whole universe by his death on the cross.

Isaac the Syrian's explicit teaching on universal salvation elicits an inevitable question: what is the sense of the whole drama of human history, if both good and evil are ultimately to be found on an equal footing in the face of God's mercy? What is the sense of suffering, ascetic labour, and prayer, if sooner or later sinners will be equated with the righteous? In how far, moreover, do Isaac's opinions correspond to the general christian tradition and to the teaching of the Gospel, in particular, to the Parable of the Last Judgment and its separation of the 'sheep' from the 'goats'?

First, when Isaac speaks about the absence of a middle realm between gehenna and the kingdom of heaven, he does not deny the reality of the separation of sheep from goats, and he even explicitly refers to it. But his attention is directed far beyond this separation, which he does not regard as final or irreversible. The Last Judgment is something which Isaac recommends people ponder on every day, and the separation of a sinner from his fellow human beings is an experience clearly depicted by Isaac when he speaks of the Judgment. His main point, however, is that the present life is the time when the separation takes place, and the Last Judgment will only reveal what spiritual state a person reached during his lifetime. Thus the Parable should not be understood as a dogmatic statement on the final destiny of the righteous and sinners, but as a prophetic warning against not having and manifesting love for one's fellows during this earthly life.

Secondly, Isaac warns that the torment of gehenna, even though limited in duration, is terrible and unbearable. He never denies the awful reality of gehenna. Yet he understands it within the context of the Gospel's message of God's unspeakable love and boundless mercy. God, in Isaac's teaching, is primarily the householder who rewards equally those who worked only one hour and those who have borne the burden and heat of the whole day. A place in the kingdom of heaven is given to a person, not on the basis of his worthiness or unworthiness, but on the basis of God's mercy and love for humankind. The kingdom of heaven is not a reward, and gehenna is not a requital: both are gifts of the merciful God 'who desires all men to be saved and to come to the knowledge of the truth'.

Thirdly, Isaac's eschatological opinions stand in the line of the teachings of such ancient Fathers as Theodore of Mopsuestia, Diodore of Tarsus, and Gregory of Nyssa. It would not be just to say, however, that he simply borrowed the ideas of his predecessors and inserted them into his own writings. Isaac's eschatological optimism and his belief in universal salvation are ultimately the result of his personal theological vision, the central conviction of which is that God is love. Around this idea his whole theological system is shaped.

Finally, the theological system of Isaac the Syrian is based on his direct experience of the mystical union with the love of God. This experience precludes any possibility of envy of other human beings, even those who have reached a higher spiritual state and thus have a chance of receiving a higher place in the kingdom of heaven. The experience of union with God as love is in itself so filled with delight that it is not for the sake of any future reward that a person prays, suffers, and toils in ascetical labours: in this very suffering, in this very prayer and ascetical labour, is concealed the experience of encounter with God. The reason for praying, bearing afflictions, and keeping the commandments is not to leave other persons behind by one's strivings or to obtain in the age to come a place that is higher than theirs. The sole reason for all ascetic toil is to experience the grace of God which is acquired through them. An encounter with God, a direct mystical experience of the divine love which one receives during one's lifetime is, for Isaac, the only justification for all struggles and efforts.

Manufactured by Amazon.ca
Bolton, ON

46678978R00076